Victory's Children

Hastings 1945-2010

by

Victoria Seymour

First published in 2010 By Victoria Seymour.

Copyright ©Victoria Seymour.

Email: mail@victoriaseymour.com

Website: www.victoriaseymour.com

ISBN 978-0-9543901-8-1

Victoria Seymour has asserted her right to be identified as the author of this work. No part of this publication may be produced, transmitted or stored in a retrieval system in any form or by any means without the written permission of the publishers.

A catalogue record of this book is available from the British Library.

Printed in Great Britain by

impression IT
Unit 2
Maunsell Road,
St Leonards-on-Sea,
East Sussex.
TN38 9NL
www.impressionit.co.uk

This book is dedicated to my daughters Barbara and Trish

My sincere gratitude goes go to the following for contributing their memories and other material to this book:

The Victory "Children": Maureen Charlesworth, Deeday White, Andre Palfrey-Martin, Dorothy and Clive Morris, John Whatman, Michael Bristow-Smith, Richard Pitcairn Knowles, Gillian Kemp, Keith Cook, Ron Burkin, Joyce Brewer, Pat and Clive Upton, Jana Tanner, Margaret Ball, Moya Frost, Ron Fellows, Conifer Rowland, Jimmy "Toller" Adams, Mark Rickman, Pam Eaves, Ruby Henderson, Joan Holt, Mary Palmer, Don Samways, Marilyn Saklatvala, Peter Moon and George Ivan Barnett. Thanks go to the families of The Late Monica Hoad, Stella Blomfield and Ivor White

Other contributors are Brian Lawes, David Padgham, Colin Smart, Eric Hughes, Philip Elms "Carole", Keith Cowper, Martin King, Paddy Manning, Patsy Haste, Paschal McCann and Thierry Zbinden.

I am indebted to Ore Village Library staff for organising a research event to further the progress of this book and to Hastings Library for a similar event and for the assistance of their reference section with historical material and photographs, Hastings Town Hall staff, Helen Bird and Roger Fuller for providing historic mayoral records and the opportunity to take photographs.

Thanks to Services to the Author by Earlyworks Press
www.earlyworkspress.co.uk

Bibliography and Web Sources

The Hastings and St Leonards Observer Archive

Martin F Mace "Sussex Wartime Relic and Memorials Wrecks, Relic and Memorials from Sussex at War 1939-1945" 1-901313-01-8

HAARG Journal Edition No 8 1999

Martin Gilbert "The Boys" ISBN 0-75380-032-2 and "The Righteous: The Unsung Heroes of the Holocaust" ISBN 0-552-99850-8

1066 Hastings Online

Horntye Park Sports Centre online history

Peter Hibbs of "The Defence of East Sussex Project" website: http://www.pillbox.org.uk/

The copyright of the post-war aerial photo of Hastings Town Centre was originally held by Photo-Precision Ltd St Albans. It is reproduced here from "Priory Meadow and the Town Centre," published by Hastings Modern History Workshop.

Every effort has been made to trace and seek holders of copyrights. Any inadvertent omissions of acknowledgement or permission will be rectified in future editions.

Opinions expressed in this book are not necessarily those of the author.

Maureen Charlesworth, Mayor of Hastings 2006-2010

I am honoured to be invited to write the foreword to this book.

I feel it is very important that a record should be made of the history of people who, like me, lived through World War Two and the hardships that followed. Although in childhood we enjoyed a freedom to roam that seems to be denied today's children, we did not have their material benefits but seem none the worse for that.

We developed a respect for and a desire to support others, qualities which, I believe, characterise the children of the 1945 victories. Proof of this is in the age group which now gives its time and energy to so many charities, beneficent organisations and clubs.

This truly is a wonderful country, with many very special people living in it.

God Bless,
Maureen Charlesworth
Mayor of Hastings

8th June, 1946

TO-DAY, AS WE CELEBRATE VICTORY, I send this personal message to you and all other boys and girls at school. For you have shared in the hardships and dangers of a total war and you have shared no less in the triumph of the Allied Nations.

I know you will always feel proud to belong to a country which was capable of such supreme effort; proud, too, of parents and elder brothers and sisters who by their courage, endurance and enterprise brought victory. May these qualities be yours as you grow up and join in the common effort to establish among the nations of the world unity and peace.

George R.I.

Prologue

Victoria Seymour

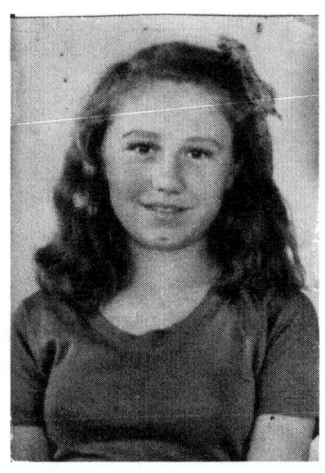

Victoria Seymour May 1945

The Taste of Victory: Jam Sandwiches Without Butter

The 1940s was a particularly restless period for my family, connected not only to the effects of war but also to my parent's work as part time domestic servants and live-in caretakers for the well-off who, during the war, had fled their homes near London for less dangerous parts of the country. In the winter of 1944 my parents finally obtained a permanent position as cook and gardener with a comfortably-off family. We left our rented semi to live in a tied cottage in the employer's grounds. My mother kept house and cooked for the family and my father cared for the gardens and greenhouses, as well as doing all the other outside work. Each day I made what seemed to me a long bus journey, to attend the school near my previous home. It was there in April 1945 that I joined in my classmates' glee at the news of Hitler's death. (I recall that "You are worse than Hitler" was the ultimate insult from children during the war.)

My new home was situated in an area that was far too posh to hold VE Day street parties. There were probably dances and dinners but I knew nothing of these. I did return to my former street to attend a party and even gate-crashed a few in nearby roads. This was not for the food; places at the tables were strictly allocated and there were watchful parents, making sure that it was only 'our kids' who enjoyed the modest spread. I went along for the sheer joy of being with a happy crowd, singing, dancing and playing games in the streets where, less than a year before, we had run in terror to shelter from V1 rockets. The church I attended also organised a street party for parishioners' children. The party fare was simple but the jam sandwiches were memorable. One mother had a stock of plum jam, which was spread thickly on unbuttered door-steps of bread; butter and margarine were too strictly rationed to allow both jam and butter on bread. Later, the church organised a coach excursion to celebrate VJ Day, with food provided; more of the butterless jam sandwiches, packed in a laundry basket lined with old sheets. On the way home we were told there was still some food left; making a roadside stop, the driver unloaded the basket and the children dived into the jam-stained sheets, clearing every crust.

During the war, from my juvenile point of view, time consisted of two periods: 'before the war' and 'after the war', with the 'after' promising to be a time when people could eat as much as they wanted of whatever they fancied. I remember that gammon rashers with three fried eggs loomed large in my father's post-war expectations. It was years before he could indulge this fancy, and by then indigestion had set in.

In 1948 my family made yet another move, from Chislehurst, near London, to a live-in job on a dairy farm at Fairlight, Hastings. This move immediately improved our living standards as far as food was concerned and, decades later, set me on the road to becoming a writer. The Hastings I discovered in the spring of 1948 was still badly scarred by war damage. I had come to accept the sight of bombed buildings as a normal part of the landscape, but it was shocking to see this picturesque town blemished by ugly gaps between the houses. Regardless of this, to my thirteen and a half year-old perception, Hastings promised the never-before-experienced delights of the seaside.

January 1945

A visitor from America in the winter of 1945 found Great Britain to be: *"A dreary place, with a serious shortage of clothing, heating, electricity and coal; the population is poorly clad and shod and has an almost obsessive preoccupation with food and how to get it."* Hastings, in spite of the grim conditions, honoured the custom of marking the New Year with children's pantomimes and official parties. The various emergency bodies set up for defence on the home front had assumed, along with their grimmer responsibilities, the role of charitable and social organisations; the air raid wardens laid on a tea party for local children and civil defence workers performed a pantomime. Even Hastings Police joined in the business of New Year entertainment; their divisional choir, under the baton of police officer Mr Vincent Batts, paid visits to local hospitals. During the first week of January, the police choir generously performed 15 pieces at the Buchanan Hospital and 20 at the Royal East Sussex Hospital, with a concert promised for St Helen's Hospital. The local newspaper, the Hastings and St Leonards Observer, said: *"They gave great pleasure to the patients and staff on duty."*

The subject of food supplies kept Hastings' councillors in long discussion in early January, when it was announced that approval had been given to a recommendation that Ferrari's Restaurant, at 58 Havelock Road, (the site now occupied by the Logie Baird Public House), unoccupied since its Italian owners were interned, should be hired for use as a British Restaurant, at a cost of £350 PA for rent and rates. The restaurant could accommodate 120 and would be able to serve 2,100 meals per week. British Restaurants were communal kitchens created during the Second World War to ensure that communities and individuals who had run out of ration coupons were still able to eat. Originally these establishments were called *"Community Feeding Centres"*; a competition was held subsequently to find a more appetizing name. A Hastings wit came up with Plate-oh's but nationally, the name British Restaurant won the day. The restaurants were set up by the Ministry of Food and run by local committees on a non-profit making basis. Meals were purchased for a set price of 9d, (4p) equivalent to £1 today. No meal could consist of more than one portion of meat, fish, eggs, or cheese. Commercial restaurants in the UK were not subject to rationing but some restrictions were placed on them, for instance, no meal could be more than three courses and the maximum price was five shillings (25p) or £5 in current buying power.

By mid-1941, over 200 British Restaurants existed in the London area; a wartime social survey conducted in 1942-43 indicated they were more popular there than in the rest of the country. Some smaller places did not qualify for a British Restaurant but instead had what was termed a *"Cash and Carry Restaurant"*, with the previously cooked meals being delivered from a British Restaurant kitchen in the area. Victoria Seymour recalls going to the British Restaurant in her village in Kent: *"It was functioning in a closed-down shoe shop, near the church and school; I think the food was delivered already cooked, from a local centre. Diners sat on long wooden benches placed in front of bare trestle tables borrowed from the school across the road. I would hand over my pennies for a substantial meal: shepherd's pie, gristly meat stews or boiled potatoes with corned beef, beetroot and shredded cabbage salad. There were 'afters': suet, steamed, or milk puddings with jam or syrup. Very basic menus, but to a hungry and cold six-year-old anything would taste good. Frequently there were no pennies at home to spare for a meal but the kindly restaurant supervisor would let me sit at the table to eat my packed lunch, often providing a free cup of cocoa to warm me up."*

During a long and heated debate over the new use of Ferrari's Restaurant Councillor Honnor proposed that the report be moved back, saying that there was no necessity for the restaurant; there were already 14 cafes in the immediate area and these were by no means working to their full capacity; more canteens were needed in the West Hill, Mount Pleasant and Hollington areas. *"I know of one town centre cafeteria with the capacity to provide 300 meals per day but only 100 are being served. A working man can get a meal there for only sevenpence, (3p) with a wide variety of choices."* Several councillors raised the needs of locals against those of seasonal visitors; a system of priority meal tickets for residents was suggested at one point. In early February the proposal was defeated and the application by Hastings Corporation for a catering licence for the proposed British Restaurant was refused. By the September of 1946, Ferrari's Restaurant was back in business, even holding wedding receptions, albeit under the government restrictions of no more than 50 guests and not much bread; by July 1946 this too had joined the list of rationed foods.

~~V~~

As a welcome distraction from the problems of food supply, the council turned its attention to a more pleasing matter: Miss H M Turner, a cousin to J M Turner, the famous landscape artist (1775-1951), gave the town a collection of objets d'art, furniture, pictures and other articles, many of which she inherited from her famous relative. She suggested in a letter to Hastings Mayor, Dr Jameson JP, that the furniture might be used in the town hall. Miss Turner's letter was read out at a town council meeting on 2nd January 1945. *"As a cousin of Mr Turner, the famous artist, I was fortunate in inheriting a number of pictures etc from his home. The chief hobby of my mother and myself has been to add to our museum and library. With increasing age and failing health, I have now decided to give the collection away. Some items have gone to the British Museum, the Tate Gallery and the Maritime Museum at Greenwich. It now gives me great pleasure to offer the remainder to Hastings for the benefit of the museum, library and education, etc. I am making no conditions except should you decide to sell anything you will undertake to use the proceeds for the benefit of the particular department to which they have been allocated. The furniture consists of Mr Turner's sideboard, wine cooler, chairs etc, which it gives me great pleasure to offer to the borough in the hope they will used in the mayor's parlour. I am sure that record will be made in the council's minutes of the historic connection so that future generations may retain and preserve these relics."*
Miss Turner's collection was intriguing; ivories, porcelain and old glass, harness brasses of different types, books, pictures and furniture. There was a tremendous number of historical items including firearms, powder flasks and other weapons, geological specimens and many other smaller objects, collected by Miss Turner in her travels. Among these were footwear of all nations, silver items, old seals and jewellery, some quite valuable, an old water clock and ancient watches.

In April 1987, a local *"Antiques Road Show"* was organised by the Hastings charity fundraiser, Jane Amstad, to benefit survivors of the Zeebrugge ferry disaster and their families. It was then that the true value of the Turner chairs and wine coolers in the mayor's parlour came to light. Michael Shorthall, of Phillips South East, who conducted the event, said that the chairs were an astonishing find and although the council had them insured for around £6,000 they were probably worth ten times that amount; the council hurriedly reviewed security at the town hall. The two wine coolers, which Mr Shorthall estimated at being worth £20,000, were also under-insured. Council Officer Ian Bear said the chairs were a very specialist item, and even Sotheby's would be surprised by the price they would secure. A plaque to commemorate Miss Turner's gift is displayed on the wall of the mayor's parlour, above the sideboard and wine coolers mentioned in her letter. The set of chairs are also part of the room's furnishings.

~~V~~

A new film-making talent emerged in Hastings during the war, in the person of George Ivan Barnett, who was born in 1925. He formed the GIB Film Club the day before war was declared. In 1941 Barnett made a patriotic feature called *"There'll Always be an England"*, in which he used shots of Hastings civil defence and fire fighters at work a thirty-minute film, costing £20, it was checked by wartime censorship authorities throughout its progress. In 1942 Barnett directed and produced a film depicting a full-scale, military attack on Hastings; a mock invasion was mounted and the Ridge was used as a stronghold defended by armed troops, with locals playing the parts of German soldiers and fleeing civilians. In 1945 Barnett tackled a more theatrical subject. An Observer reporter, visiting the GIB club studio at 68, Norman Road St Leonards, said that he was taken back to the picturesque and exciting days of the 14th Century, when he witnessed the filming of the club's latest production, *"The Manor House"*, under the direction of Barnett, whose day job was as a camera operator, employed by the Gaumont-British Corporation at Hastings Ritz Cinema. The Observer reporter wrote: *"On a realistic set representing a stone-walled room in a mediaeval mansion, a banquet scene, followed by a thrilling duel, was enacted. About 30 members of the club, in the costumes of 500 years ago, played the scenes, which were photographed in colour by Mr Barnett. Sirloins of beef, large legs of mutton, chicken and turkey presented a tempting appearance on the table, looking as if they had come straight from the oven. In reality they arrived from a theatrical props store in London. The story of " The Manor House," which was written by members of the club, tells how the hero, the lord of the manor, returns from the Crusades to find that a tyrannous baron has seized his house and land and is striving to win his betrothed. Disguised as a minstrel he enters the manor and kills the baron in a duel but is himself slain by the baron's henchmen. Gwen Watford, the gifted young actress who has appeared successfully in the Court Players, has the role of the heroine and Keith Wood plays the hero. In a prologue to the film some modern tourists are shown asking a gardener the history of an ancient tomb in the manor grounds, and from this opening the story unfolds. The stone walls of the set, looking almost as realistic as the work of mediaeval masons, are actually cardboard, made piece by piece and hand stitched by Mr Barnett's mother. Consisting of over 300 hundred pieces, the wall took two months hard work to prepare. The stone floor is also made of squares of cardboard and a large tapestry, which heightens the realism of the setting, was cleverly painted by Hugh Gladwish. The colourful mediaeval costumes were made under the skilful and experienced direction of Peter Steele, who is also in charge of general make-up. Sound track is being added by Mr Barnett's camera colleagues of the Gaumont-British Film Corporation."* In 1949 Barnett made the film *"The Fall of the House of Usher"* on a budget of £10 and in 1954 he directed and produced a feature about lighthouses; Trinity House holds a copy of this. His career as filmmaker continued into the early 1960s and he also ran a photographic studio in Trinity Passage in Hastings until 1984. George Ivan Barnett now lives in retirement in Newquay, Cornwall.

~~V~~

Councillor Ford, chairman of the Defence Areas Hotel and Catering Industry Survival Movement contributed an article to the January edition of the Drapers Record, contemplating the re-opening of hotels and boarding houses in Hastings and other seaside resorts. He supplied what he described as *"Striking figures of the quantities of household linen goods that will be required to ready these establishments for business. These estimates, which I consider reliable, may prove to be less than the actual demand. One third of the quantities quoted may be available during the year following the end of hostilities in Europe and the rest over the two years after that. The calculations are based on my long years of experience of the equipment required in the hotel business."* Ford's shopping list is not only impressive for its magnitude but also quaint for the inclusion as essentials items rarely used 65 years on: *"1,200,000 square yards carpet, 600,000 yards cloth curtains, 160,000 sheets, 800,000 rugs and mats, 120,000 blankets, 80,000 pillow cases, 80,000 bath sheets, 120,000 bath towels, 96,000 face cloths, 400,000 chair covers, 32,000 dish cloths, 40,000 bolster covers, 48,000 eiderdowns, 48,000 bedspreads, 64,000 dining table covers, 48,000 doilies and tablemats, 60,000 tablecloths, 96,000 table napkins, 48,000 mattress covers and 200,000 yards net curtaining."*

~~V~~

At the time Councillor Ford's article was published all the items he mentioned were scarce and on coupons. Interest must have been generated when, in the same edition of the Observer that carried the hotel shopping list, an advertisement appeared for a coupon-free sale of household linen and clothing. Mr A Relfe, of the Clive Vale Hat Shop, 195, Harold Road, was offering his customers a no-coupon sale of *"renovated goods."* What this euphemism meant is unclear; perhaps they were recovered stock from a bomb-damaged shop. In the list of renovated goods were a limited number of items of clothing, in seriously short supply throughout Europe. In January the Women's Voluntary Service appealed to knitters to make garments for the children of the liberated and war-torn Continent; wool and knitting patterns could be supplied on application from 42 Wellington Square. The appeal came directly from the war office; when the clothes were finished they would be distributed by the army. Hastings was fortunate that in the face of fuel and clothing shortages the snow of January 1945 was short-lived. Throughout the war, there were no weather forecasts and newspaper reports on weather conditions were held back, lest they aid the enemy. Two weeks after the event Hastings residents read in the Observer that locally the cold had been severe enough to freeze household water systems and the corporation had put stand-pipes in the street to provide a water supply for householders. The freeze was quickly followed by bright, sunny days giving the illusion of spring, as people strolled on the promenade or sat feeding the pigeons.

~~V~~

Miss Sheila Kaye-Smith, a popular local novelist, spoke to the Rotary Club at the Ritz Cinema in January on the subject of *"Town and Country."* In a talk that in part resonates with today she said: *"People talk of Hastings as a holiday resort and a pleasure town but Hastings is also very much a place of work. It has much to identify of its own, apart from the visitors and the tourist traffic. During the wartime evacuation period and the time of the tip and run raids, Hastings seemed more alive than most of its neighbours. The life of the town went on and it seemed to be able to maintain itself much more vigorously than other towns of the kind. The reason for this is that Hastings is not just a pleasure resort. It has always had a life of its own, apart from its character as a holiday resort. When the holiday makers and tourist traffic disappears it is a town that is likely to return more quickly to itself. What gives the identity and vitality to a place is its work. Therefore, if we rob the country of its main industry of fishing, farming and agriculture and use it for pleasure only, we are taking something from the country and*

England itself." Miss Kaye-Smith's regional novels are set in the borders of Sussex and Kent and her work is characterized by its preoccupation with 19th Century rural concerns and the effects of industrialisation on the countryside and provincial life. Hastings features in her book *"Tamarisk Town,"* under the name *"Marlingate."*

February 1945

Hastings Councillor Alderman Tingle opened up controversy by saying that when the war was over Hastings Council would purchase Morrison shelters from householders. Observer readers were quick to reach for their pens:

"I am informed by the Borough Engineers Department that the council will not be buying back Morrison shelters. I have been in communication with the Ministry of Home Security and our Member of Parliament on the matter and I was informed that the re-purchase was not contemplated. The question of paying for shelters when they were first distributed appears to me to be wrong; the council should consider re-purchasing, should the present owners desire it. I am not suggesting the full amount of £7 should be refunded but only a reasonable proportion. According to the newspapers the present value of a Morrison shelter varies between £5 and nothing. In common with Alderman Tingle I was led to believe that I should be able to re-sell my shelter to the council. R S Woods Fairlight Avenue Hastings

Would these people who expect to get money back from the council have had a Morrison shelter if they realised at the time that the government would not be prepared to buy them back? Did they not think, in common with thousands, that £7 they were paying was good insurance and a means of saving their lives? It is beyond a joke when government officials, who have more important work on their hands, are pestered by people who want a few miserable pounds refunded. Rather let them rejoice that they had a Morrison shelter and put their energies into making sure they are never needed again. They should remember that those who built themselves permanent shelters at their own expense are not crying out for reimbursement. Edward J Avery 10 Coventry Road St Leonards."

Another correspondent, calling himself a building operative, came up with a public use for the unwanted Morrison shelters: *"There seems to be rather a heated argument regarding Morrison shelters, with no apparent solution as to what to do with them. To my mind they would make very good bus shelters. Elevate the steel roof by using the angle irons... The height of the shelter can be adjusted by welding the base angle irons to any desired length... Tensile strength for the structure can be added wherever necessary.*

These structures can be removed during the summer months and stored, ready for winter. As to labour, we have our evening classes and the young engineers need training. If this idea is a washout, surely somebody has good suggestion for utilizing the Morrison shelters."

The Morrison shelter was a double bed sized, steel-framed self-assembly cage with a sheet steel top. When a mattress was placed inside, it allowed no upright sitting space for adults. The base of the shelter material was metal mesh, as were the end and side panels. Two-tier shelters were supplied for larger families or where it was inappropriate for house occupants to share a bed. Over 500,000 Morrison shelters were delivered to British households by November 1941, an additional 100,000 were ordered in late 1943, and 9,000 were distributed to London residents as late as January and February 1944. Morrison shelters were supplied free to families earning less than £350 per year and £7 to those earning more. Victoria Seymour said: *"As far as I recall my family got a Morrison shelter in 1944; it was the two-tier version, as we were a family of four. It sat in the corner of our small living room, next to the fireplace. It was too high for use as a table so it became a shelf on which all manner of things were dumped for the duration of the war. Prior to this we had no shelter at all so every time there was an air raid in the night I had to be woken up and pushed, protesting, into next door's draughty, brick-built surface-standing shelter, which in fact offered little protection from anything other than blast. It was from there we witnessed the first night of the doodlebugs, fearful and mystified, as was the entire south east England population that night, by these noisy 'planes on fire.' With the arrival in our home of a Morrison shelter my bedtime routine changed; there was no more being sent upstairs and I snuggled down to sleep early, with family life going round me, just what most young children want. The problem of disposing of the Morrison was not ours as we moved house before the war was over."*

Morrison shelters were certainly effective: a survey of the performance of 44 heavily damaged houses with the shelters installed showed that without them the occupants would probably have been killed. Direct hits on the shelter by a bomb accounted for most fatalities; although a proportion of fatalities occurred where the shelter had not been correctly sited in the residence. The other form of civilian shelter that became redundant was the Anderson. Over two million of these were supplied during the war; they were cheap to produce and provided free-of-charge to those households with a garden and where the occupying family earned less than £250 per year. The curved steel sections of the Anderson Shelter were relatively simple to construct. When completed, it was set in a rectangular hole and the waste soil used to cover the shelter, giving increased protection from the effects of bomb-blast. The Anderson shelters were often cold, damp and prone to flooding, particularly during winter, but they were very effective and saved many lives.

The government set about recovering the shelters that had been supplied free of charge. Householders were told to dismantle them and store the components until they could be collected. Boy Scouts were mobilized to assist households with no able-bodied men, a high proportion at that time. Anyone wishing to keep their shelter could purchase it at a modest cost: £1 for an Anderson and £1-10s-0d (£1.50) for a Morrison. Thousands took up this offer and, in the face of the serious post-war shortage of construction materials, sections of the shelters were used as fencing or to make hutches and runs for small domestic animals. The Anderson shelter, after being unearthed and set on a brick base, served as a bicycle or tool shed. On farms and workshops the steel roofs of the Morrison shelters were used for flooring and the uprights as supports for work benches, some of which are still in use today. The demolition of surface-standing, brick shelters certainly helped one man: A Mr Johnson wanted to extend his garage but building materials were very difficult to obtain. He asked his local council if he could purchase the bricks from the shelters. The council agreed but warned him that he was unlikely to find many in a usable condition. Mr Johnson was no fool; he had examined the shelters and realized that the quality of the mortar was very poor. He ended up with 31,000 bricks in almost perfect condition for a token payment. Underground public and communal shelters were closed immediately after V.E. day and eventually filled in. The road blocks and blast walls that were installed to obstruct invasion vehicles and protect people and buildings were demolished even before the war ended. A local resident, Mrs Kingham of 2 Cornwallis Gardens, came up with an idea for reusing waste wood: *"It is puzzling one to know what the corporation intend doing with the timber that has been used for indoor protection from air raids. While it served a good purpose indoors it is now doing anything but; either it leans on the house or is put on the garden path. If no other use can be found for this timber cannot the householder buy it? With the threatened shortage of winter fuel this would keep the home fires burning and, incidentally, provide a little revenue for the Corporation."* The demolition gangs clearing the bomb sites had already found their own way of recycling the timber from wrecked houses. Joyce Brewer, a former wartime milk round worker, recalls: *"The men put the wood in a separate pile and people were invited to help themselves. I took away a lot of wood in my milk van, for my family and others."*

~~V~~

February was the month during which Hastings Police Superintendent Knell made his official report to the Licensing Justices on the previous year's convictions for drunkenness figures. He was careful to point out that, while the figures, eight cases in all, were low, allowances should be made for the conditions existing in the town during the year under review: Many pubs were closed, there was a shortage of alcohol and the population had been reduced by evacuation and from May 1944 there were fewer service personnel in town. The editor of the Hastings Observer, Frederick Goodsell, who under the pseudonym *"Vigilant",* wrote the column *"Flotsam and Jetsam",* had his say on the subject: *"I have no doubt it will be noted that the eight persons convicted were non-residents. While this is a tribute to the sobriety of the townspeople, it may equally well be taken as a reflection of the hard times through which the population has been passing; few people are likely to be able to afford excessive indulgence in liquor at present prices. Superintendent Knell records that the majority of licensed houses are well conducted and that every effort is made by landlords to carry on in their business in a proper manner. He refers to their difficulties over staff and supply shortages and his general summing up is that the town's record in the sphere of the licensed trade is very good. I would express the confident hope it will never be otherwise."*

Goodsell's weekly feature gave him an opportunity to express his personal opinion on events in Hastings and the wider world. He had joined the staff of the Observer in 1926, as a cub reporter. His abilities were recognised early, and on the 1940 retirement of the paper's editor, Sir Alfred Dyer, Goodsell succeeded him, aged only 31. In print he appears be stuffy and pompous by today's standards, but retired Observer reporter, Philip Elms, former Observer sub-editor, has said of Goodsell: *"He believed passionately in Hastings and ensured the Observer's coverage was thorough and meaningful. You could read his paper years later and get a fair understanding of the town's lifestyle. Goodsell was among the last of his breed."* Those colleagues who knew him in his latter years said that at work Goodsell was opinionated, controlling and bad-tempered, possibly due to his fondness for the whisky he kept in his office. He had old-fashioned principles, offering to resign as editor should the owners of the Observer consider making pictures of pretty girls a feature in the newspaper. Don Samways, who started work as an apprentice reporter in 1948, said: *"Goodsell was a remote figure and looked upon as a god in the office. I recall that another revered employee of the Observer office at that time was Dolly Swaine, with whom Goodsell appeared to have a good working relationship."*

~~V~~

On Monday 12th February rumours were circulating in Hastings that a buried bomb, a relic of the Battle of Britain, had exploded in Milward Road. This fear proved unfounded, as a Hastings Observer report tells: *"About 30 feet of the Castle Hill Road end of Milward Road, which is said to have been unsafe for a considerable period, gave way, slid down a steep bank and over the wall into Stonefield Road. No one was hurt. Mrs Jenner, of 14 Stonefield Road, who lives opposite the scene of the slide, said that she was upstairs in the front room, when she happened to look out of the window, to see the wall gradually crumble and great pieces of concrete, with bricks and lengths of railings, slide slowly down the bank. A long garden wall at 16, Albany Road, the property of Mrs Marson, Spring Mount, Upper Maze Hill, St Leonards, crumbled a few days before this event and a similar incident occurred elsewhere in Albany Road. Theories advanced to account for the collapse of the two walls in St Leonards include the aftermath of blast, the recent severe frosts or a slight earth tremor."*

~~V~~

"Vigilant", a keen supporter of cricket, commented on the future of Hastings Central Cricket Ground, assuring readers its future was still safe: *"I noticed, by the way, when recently looking through the current issue of the "Cricketer Annual," that publicity was given to an entirely erroneous notion about the future of the Central Ground. In a feature headed "Preston's Diary", reference is made to the ground being considered an ideal position for a new town hall for which, according to the diarist, our town council is looking. I must point out here that Mr Preston is bowling very wide of the wicket. Apparently his comments are based on a hazy idea of a remark made by Councillor F S Bouquet, during a discussion on the town hall scheme, which failed to secure the council's approval last year. It was tentatively suggested by Councillor Bouquet that the ideal site was South Terrace, facing the Central Ground, which he thought might be transformed into a*

central "place", adorned by a statue of Mr Churchill. So Mr Preston's concluding remark that Sussex may not play there any more is quite without foundation, as, indeed, the match now arranged for July, shows. It is a pity that he did not verify his references. As a matter of fact, I believe that under the terms of the trust deed governing the Central Ground, any possibility that it could ever be converted from its present use is extremely remote, if not entirely illusory. And this is all to the good, because the existence of this wide green space, devoted to a traditional English game, in the very centre of Hastings, easily accessible to all forms of transport, has surely been of no small value to the town's past, and is likely to remain so in the future, whatever plans are made for post-war development."

The strongly held belief in the cricket ground being sacrosanct was tested in 1983, when proposals to develop the Central Cricket Ground were put forward by five different developers. After a public inquiry by the Secretary of State for the Environment, all applications were refused, on the grounds that it would create problems in relation to drainage, the roads and parking. But this was not the end of the matter; a planning brief, which addressed the issues raised by the 1983 inquiry, was approved by Hastings Borough Council in 1985. The brief outlined details for the improvement and pedestrianisation of Hastings Town Centre, the construction and development of shopping facilities, improvements to existing roadways and the additional pedestrianisation of other areas. In 1987, planning permission for the proposed shops was granted and in 1988 a plan put forward by developer, Speyhawk was upheld and compulsory purchase orders were confirmed. However, recession brought the proposed development to a halt. Speyhawk pulled out due to lack of funds but the proposal still stood. Work began on a replacement cricket ground at Summerfields, now known as Horntye Park; the pedestrianisation of Castle Street and Wellington Place was completed at the close of 1991.

By May 1995, a new developer, Boots Properties PLC, in company with Marks and Spencer and British Home Stores, had signed contracts; a £50 million scheme and full planning application was submitted and approved by Hastings Borough Council. The scheme created deep divisions locally, between those who supported the development of the ground, and those who thought it would result in considerable historical and environmental loss for the town. It was also the latter's view that the hopes of the new shopping centre bringing financial assistance to the flagging local economy were without foundation and that a standard format shopping centre, with famous

High Street names, was not the way to revive tourism. The opposing standpoint was that the development would revive declining tourism and boost the local economy. While agreeing that the loss of the Central Cricket and Recreation Ground was a great pity, they believed that, due to the ground's financial situation, its closure was inevitable. On 6th June 1997, Queen Elizabeth officially declared open Hastings' new Priory Meadow Shopping Centre; there was no statue of Winston Churchill to *"adorn the place."* Instead, in the part of the shopping centre known as Queen's Square, Her Majesty unveiled a bronze statue of a cricketer, a memento of the 130 years of cricket played on a unique, town centre, below sea-level ground. A potted history of the piece of land on which the cricket ground stood puts the controversy into perspective: In 1864 the ground was developed and in 1872 it was placed under a Trust Deed; cricket was played on the ground henceforth. Over the years the open space was used as a recreation area for the townspeople, for circuses, the hustings, various sports and even the landing of a balloon. The Horntye Sports Centre holds archive of the Central Cricket Ground's records; scorebooks, historical photographs, including those of famous sportsmen who have played at Hastings, an extensive library and items of memorabilia.

March 1945

Prior to the arrival of Easter visitors, the Food Control Committee worked on the problems arising from the expected influx; mainly the granting of licences to catering establishments and the difficulties of staffing Hastings cafes and restaurants. There was a chronic shortage of catering staff, brought about by the Ministry of Labour's policy of directing workers away from the area, to be employed in vital war work. The war effort also required trained caterers for the canteens of factories and other essential establishments, thus draining coastal resorts of such workers. Although resented, the direction of labour scheme had the unintended effect of providing workers with better paid jobs and created reluctance in those directed away from coastal towns to return to the lower paid jobs in seasonal catering.

Hastings workmen set about repairing sea-battered beach groynes, a sight so unusual that crowds gathered to watch. The re-opening of Hastings Pier was considered in 1945 but it was decided this was out of the question for at least one, if not two years, as the pier was not de-requisitioned and a small government rent was still being paid for it. During WWII the pier was breached to prevent it from being used as a landing stage in the event of an enemy invasion. *"Vigilant"* used the subject as a topic for his column: *"The public are wondering how soon it will be possible for the pier to resume its functions as an entertainments centre. But that is a matter for the Pier Company to decide in the light of wartime circumstances. From the town's viewpoint the sooner the pier is in working order the better."* (The pier, though still bomb-damaged, was derequisitioned and opened in 1946 and, as far as possible, resumed its role as a holiday attraction, with dances, angling competitions, performances in its little theatre and the popular amusement arcade.)

~~V~~

Hastings and St Leonards' visitor accommodation was fully booked for Easter 1945, with many finding alternative beds in private houses. There was a hope that the wartime holiday would provide a curtain-raiser to the first season that Hastings and St Leonards had known since August 1939. These hopes were met when the holiday brought a total of 20,000 rail arrivals; buses transported hundreds of others to the bomb-scarred town, which did its best to re-create the spirit of peacetime Bank Holidays. The Hastings Observer reported: *"It was a very prosperous Eastertide, which fully realised optimistic forecasts. It has given encouragement in all quarters to expect a successful 'Victory Holiday' season this summer, which will, it is hoped, do much to set the town on the road to regaining the astounding popularity that its pre-war enterprise had built up. Although one day of the holiday, Sunday, was wet, for most of the time weather conditions were favourable, with some sunshine to temper the departing winds of March."*

~~V~~

There was a mood to be rid of emergency defence buildings, such as gun emplacements, pill boxes and air raid shelters, as quickly as possible. With a lack of manpower much clearance of these installations had to be postponed, in some cases for years. The nation's main task was to rebuild and repair its housing stock, a subject that filled the letters columns of local and national newspapers in the months leading up to victory and for years after.

"After four years of hardship we apartment landlords have a chance of making up arrears. Business is good, even without expensive advertising, but what is the council or powers responsible going to do about war damage repairs? Take my case out of numbers; seven rooms and only three fit to let. I have been waiting for three months for roof repairs, etc. The builders are kept so short-staffed they are helpless in the matter. As Hastings and St Leonards depend mostly on visitors for revenue, something will have to done quickly or half the place will be bankrupt.
M Gibbs, 25, Stockleigh Road, St Leonards"

"Mrs Gibbs is fortunate in waiting three months only for repairs to her house. We have been waiting four and a half years. Our two sunny rooms were wrecked on 10th September 1940 and are still unrepaired. In March 1943 the rest of the ceilings fell down and windows were broken and the entire top floor is still uninhabitable, owing to another bomb. Draughts, damp and dust cause much discomfort. We are patiently waiting for workmen in vain. Visitors welcome to see the ruins.
G Ward. Green Hayes, 46, Springfield Road."

"I am a resident of Hastings and St Leonards and a great admirer of the towns and the way they have carried on in the difficult days of the war. However, a young friend of mine has been looking for a flat or small house for herself and her two small boys and has heard many times, when enquiring, that she could not be taken in as they could not have children in the flats because they would disturb the old people, who must be considered in every way. This seems a pretty poor reward for fighting men, who have defended their country and these same old people, to find that they and their wives and children are not wanted by some in this town. No wonder the birth rate is going down and children are being neglected, due to the awful strain being imposed on young mothers, who have to face the responsibility alone. This attitude is not worthy of Hastings and its wonderful traditions and this blot on the escutcheon must be erased. With apologies for writing in this way but I feel very deeply about the matter.
A MOTHER"

Another reader recounted her experience in trying to buy a house: *"One was advertised and my daughter and I went to the sale. The house when built cost £675. The auctioneer started the bidding at £1000 and in a minute or two the bidding rose to £1,970. He then asked, "Have you all done, can't I have another ten pounds?' Nobody replied and the house went for that huge sum. The Minister of Housing was wrong when he said in Parliament that he is sure there is no profiteering in the sale of houses."*

~~V~~

With the passage of 65 years the majority of wartime emergency structures have disappeared in Hastings and elsewhere. Some historically prominent installations form part of museums or visitor attractions, for example: at Newhaven, where a former Victorian fort overlooking the sea has many WWII gun batteries. At Dover cliff-set WWII operations rooms draw thousand of visitors every year. Relics of small defence buildings are still to be found at roadsides or on public footpaths and common land; others decay unnoticed in copses and fields on private property. It is not just buildings that remain; on some of the remoter military sites in Britain, parts of rusting military vehicles, war machinery, and even live ammunition can be found, the latter presenting real danger to the unwary.

The Hastings area has a few WWII installations; still standing is a cluster of *"dragon's teeth"*, (rectangular, concrete tank traps), on the beach at

Bulverhythe and Rock-a-Nore. At the time of writing there stands on the Stade a red-painted WWII mine, used as a charity collection box. Sited under the Torfield allotments is a large public air raid shelter, the only tangible evidence of its existence being a ventilation pipe, rising from the grassy area bordering the rows of vegetables. There are other buried air raid shelters around the town: An Internet group, the self-styled *"Urban Explorers"*, recently took photographs inside a closed-down Hastings underground shelter. The images show that the walls stand firm and, for the most part, the place appears dry. The rusting metal frame of a folding bed and dented aluminium household utensils suggest the shelter may have been used as a dwelling for vagrants, before its entrance was bricked up. In the darkness, enormous white spiders thrive.

At Pett Level there are the remains of an emergency coastal battery situated on Toot Rock, overlooking the beaches and a nature reserve. The battery consists of the gun house, observation post, mortar sites and other features, rendering it self-contained when under attack. After Dunkirk and the retreat of Allied Forces from France, the threat of German invasion brought about an intensive building programme of coastal defences such as the one at Pett Level. The purpose of these structures was purely utilitarian, each built to a standard design, with immensely thick concrete walls. Pett Level Beach, closed for the duration, was re-opened to the public on 31st April 1945, as were the coastal areas around Pevensey Bay, Norman's Bay and Camber. In the years following the war, local children played in the abandoned gun emplacement at Pett Level; their being forbidden to go there made it all the more exciting. Peter Hibbs provided the following comments, left by visitors to his web site: *"Carole"* wrote: *"I lived at the Coastguard Station on Toot Rock from 1946 until 1952; my sibling and I were the only children there at the time. We used to run wild, climbing up and down the ladders of the emplacement, it's a miracle we were not killed."*

Keith Cowper, born at Pett in 1941, wrote: *"During the war there were many Canadian soldiers posted on Pett Level. They all visited my grandmother's house, named "Jacques", in Pett and the soldiers adopted me as their mascot. After the war my aunt, Doreen Cooke, married one of them. I do remember the Canadians coming to the house when I was very small; they had brought a Bren gun carrier to take me for a ride. When it started up it was so noisy I screamed the place down. After the war we used to play cowboys at the gun emplacement and an old man, Mr Gostick, would chase us off because he was afraid we would mess about with the water tanks up there."*

Martin King, Pett resident, wrote: *"These water tanks supplied local houses, including the former coastguard houses on Toot Rock. During the war, the coastguard cottages, which were by then in private hands, were requisitioned by the military and used to house the personnel from the gun battery. There are some concrete structures in one of the gardens, which I believe were associated with Nissan huts, used as a canteen for troops. The battery originally had two six-inch guns but one gun position seems to have been destroyed, a house is now situated in the area where you would expect it to have been. The house standing where the second gun emplacement used to be was built out of that structure in 1959, it has amazingly thick walls. There is a patio on the seaward side and on that can be seen the place where the gun was mounted."*

During WWII, the late Stella Blomfield worked and lived at Guestling, in Snushall's, the village grocery and general store. It was part of her duties to deliver supplies to the British and Canadian soldiers camped at Pett Level; some villagers were obliged to billet soldiers, singly or in groups, others were accommodated in the hutted encampments: *"One day I arrived at the camp and absentmindedly left the key in the ignition of the van. The duty sergeant discovered my offence and said I must report to the village police constable. He gave me a telling off but my father just laughed; reminding me that when that particular constable was assigned to collect a gun from a person who did not have permission to hold it, the policeman shot himself in the foot. Like my father, the policeman had been a WWI soldier and should have known how to handle weapons. Perhaps it was a Bren gun, which was notorious for causing accidents. My memories of the victory celebrations are a little vague now. I do recall that we had no flags, so somebody strung their washing across the village green between two telegraph poles. We had a victory party in a barn-like building behind the shop where I worked; people gathered bluebells and white cow parsley to decorate the place."*

Some locals took the job of demolition of defence installations into their own hands: A farmer, Mr E. J Trythall of Key West Farm Baldslow, devised a method of disposing of a concrete tank trap. In 1940 a line of these was built across the farmer's fields and after the war he had to make a gap to get his tractor through for ploughing. His solution was to excavate a pit by the side of the block, and, after digging away at its foundations, he toppled it over and into the pit, by means of levers and a car jack. The pit to take the block measured ten feet by seven feet and was five feet deep. The work was done by Mr Trythall and a Mr R Cox, in about 26 hours. The farmer offered anyone else with a similar problem to inspect the job.

A more dramatic deconstruction took place on Hastings Seafront: Under the headline *"Flame Defence Secret Disclosed"* the Observer told that Hastings was one of the coastal towns where Britain's secret flame defence installations were sited, for use in the event of an attempted enemy invasion during the war. The report ran: *"The official release of details of this method of ensuring a hot reception for any would-be invaders makes it permissible to describe what was done in the town. It will be recalled that German plan for the invasion of England, which was seized by our own invading forces when they advanced into Belgium, indicated that Hastings was one of the places that the enemy had marked out for landing operations, as part of the assault on London. If ever the Germans had made such an attempt, a terrifying belt of flame, bursting from the sea, would have met them at Hastings and other key points along the coast. Oil from the camouflaged reservoirs, conveyed from the shore and out to sea by steel pipes and set on fire by chemical means on contact with water, would have fed the tremendous flames, as they roared on the surface of the sea all along this part of the channel. Two of the oil reservoirs, great circular steel tanks, enclosed in massive brickwork and hidden from view under camouflage netting, were built in the White Rock Gardens. Another was constructed at the Fishmarket, on the site of the children's boating lake, where other defences were also erected. Yet another was built at Rock-a Nore, under the East Hill Cliff. Men have recently been at work demolishing the White Rock reservoirs; the others were pulled down earlier in the year. The demolition work, completed by the use of oxy-hydrogen metal cutting apparatus, has been a slow and strenuous task, owing to the size and strength of the structures. The oil pipes running along the seafront, encased in brick and concrete for protection, have recently been partly removed; some of this structure still remains. Foam from the apparatus for fire fighting was also part of the installation at the Fishmarket and elsewhere. The great reservoirs, looking rather like the Martello Towers, constructed for defence in the days when Napoleon threatened England with invasion and the pipes along the seafront, must have mystified many people at Hastings during the war. Now the secret can be told."*

Some wartime installations hung on for decades: Described by the Observer in February 1971 as *"The Reluctant Shelter"* and situated in Caves Road, St Leonards, was one of the last remaining public, brick surface air raid shelters. For two weeks its 18-inch thick brick and reinforced concrete walls continued to defy repeated attempts to demolish it. Mr Reginald Dicker, proprietor of R W Dicker and Co, of Rock Lane, told an Observer reporter why it was taking so long: *"It would be uneconomical to keep men occupied there continuously so it has become a job which we are doing more or less in our free time. We have had other much more important jobs elsewhere but if the weather stops that work, we put men on the Caves Road Site. When we can get mechanical compressors and drills on the site it won't take long to get it down."* In 2010, the owner of a local recycling firm called on a house in the St Helen's area to collect. He was asked to, *"Pick up the stuff from the bottom of the garden; it's beside the air raid shelter."* The shelter proved to be a surface-built, 25 person custom model, still standing after 70 years.

Uphill work. Delivering milk by hand-cart in January 1945

Standpipes in Cornwallis Gardens, January 1945

Repairing the groynes on Hastings Beach March 1945

Removing wartime defence installations at Hastings Town Centre.
Date unknown

Hastings Easter Holiday crowds

Two of the set of six Turner Chairs in the Mayor's Parlour

April 1945

Early April brought "National Milk Bottle Recovery Week." Due to so many milk bottles being lost in enemy action, the bottle manufacturers had found it impossible to meet demands, resulting in serious shortage. Mr H R Phelps, secretary of Hastings and St Leonards' Wartime Dairy Association published a request to the public to co-operate in the campaign by collecting every bottle not in circulation, irrespective of the owner, and returning them to the nearest dairyman for redistribution. A further plea for community help came from the Salvation Army's Major Charles H Downs of Milward Road; he asked that the women of Hastings donate 300 'hussifs' to European women. *"It has been brought to our notice that hussifs are a sorely needed article of great value to Europe's mothers, whose homes are in the wake of the British Liberation Army. The ladies of Hastings Salvation Army are busy making husiffs for their post-war relief fund and gifts can be left at The Citadel, St Andrew's Square."* (Hussif is a corruption of the word housewife, in this sense being a wallet or cloth roll containing sewing threads and needles, buttons, a thimble and scissors. These were issued to all serving men so that they could repair their own clothes.)

~~V~~

On the 10th April Hastings Town Council held a final meeting at its wartime quarters in Summerfields. One of the subjects under discussion was the immediate derequisitioning of Hastings hotels and boarding houses in cases where the owners wished to regain possession of their properties and re-open them for business. It was acknowledged that a severe shortage of labour and building materials was hampering restoration work, even though hotels and guesthouses, along with private homes, had priority. By mid-April, Hastings was already laying plans for victory celebrations. To further the recovery of the town, the bus service was to be improved, with a skeleton Sunday service and a later evening timetable, in the hope of helping businesses to attract the much needed staff back to the catering and service industries. As far as the weather was concerned, contemporary reports show that in April 1945 the Sussex coast resembled a Mediterranean shore, with temperatures of 70 degrees in the shade and the beaches full of sunbathers and swimmers. Householders were reminded that war was not yet over with the warning that the five-mile coastal dim-out regulation had to remain in force, to avoid giving assistance to enemy submarines or other craft. A General Election was in the offing and the town's Conservative MP, Hely Hutchinson, stepped down in favour of the party's new candidate, ex-Irish Guardsman, Major Neil Cooper-Key.

~~V~~

"Vigilant" wrote in his column that he was sure Hastings people would be interested to learn of the transatlantic publicity that the town and its wartime ordeal had recently received: *"It is a long way from Hastings to Toronto but the Observer provides a regular link. It is sent there to Mr G R Skilton by his sister. Mr Skilton, who was employed at the Observer office more than 40 years ago, sent me a copy of the Toronto Evening Telegram, in which is reproduced the map of where wartime bombs fell in the borough, which the Observer published in the autumn of 1944. Mr Skilton took the original copy of the map along to the offices of the Evening Telegram. Over the space of five columns, the Canadian newspaper gave the map prominence, at the top of a page devoted to their War Victims Fund that has raised a total of 2,598,800 dollars up to the date of the issue. With the map is produced a summary of the air attacks on the borough, which amounted to 500 high explosive bombs being dropped here in 85 raids, killing 115 and injuring 700. A picture accompanying the article shows a group of boys and girls at a Toronto school, who had voluntarily saved five dollars for the fund by sacrificing treats, sweets and entertainments."*

~~V~~

With sad frequency throughout the war and after, the Observer carried news items on local servicemen who had been killed or were missing in action. Added to these reports as the armies progressed across Europe were accounts of released prisoners of war, among which was one of a man discovered in unusual circumstances. After nothing had been heard of him throughout the war, the American Third Army found the artist brother of a Hastings resident living in a castle he owned, near the village of Hungen, 30 miles from Frankfurt. The man was Mr James Pitcairn-Knowles, who had been living with his wife, the Italian-German Princess Louise Solms-Braunfels, who was related to the Italian royal family. Mr Pitcairn-Knowles had been told by the Germans to consider himself under arrest and was confined to his rooms all the time. His Hastings-residing brother, Andrew Pitcairn-Knowles, founder and owner of the Riposo Health Hydro on the Ridge, told the Observer that he had not seen his brother since before the war: *"I had feared he was dead because he was very anti-Hitler in his views and expressed them openly in the village; I was afraid the Gestapo might have made away with him. I am very much relieved to hear he is still alive and I now hope to get in touch with him. My brother is chiefly a portrait painter; he lived in Germany for his art and because he likes the country. He had been there since before the last war and was interned there for a while during that time. He was released from internment due to the state of his health and allowed to go to a sanatorium."* In his book "The Edwardian Eye of Andrew Pitcairn-Knowles", (an early photo-journalist who founded a German sports magazine in the late 19th century), his grandson and biographer, Richard, added more detail to the story of the liberation of his Great-Uncle James: *"The town of Hungen had reason to be grateful to James; he is still remembered for saving it from devastation by shelling, when he walked across fields towards the advancing Americans, carrying a white flag and a Union Jack, to say that the German army had left the town. The sight of an 80 year-old Englishman appearing in the front line must have been a surprise. He lived another ten years and died in his castle in 1954."*

~~V~~

There are enough of stories of the wartime exploits of Hastings fishermen to fill a book. Jimmy "Toller" Adams, ex-Royal Navy and retired Hastings fisherman, aged 80, recalled the late Malcolm Mitchell. *"There was a brick surface shelter on the Stade in WWII, with a look-out on top. Malcolm Mitchell, who was not just a fisherman but a coastguard, would station himself there to see if anything suspicious was taking place."* Malcolm had been in the Royal Navy in the First World War; his thoughts on the ending of WWII are not recorded but in its aftermath he founded a business that served as a reminder of war, trading for over 40 years in Hastings Old Town. A government War Department surplus store, its cramped premises housed piles of what to the uninitiated looked like junk. Malcolm had originally run a marine store from 7, High Street but in 1946 he opened his new business at number 48, a former draper's, (in 1940, its cellar had briefly been a Methodist Chapel.) Malcolm's brothers, Tom and Jim, worked with him and lived over the shop. Jimmy Adams said: *"The stock was partly job lots collected from the naval dockyards at Portsmouth, Chatham and Devonport; it was just pot luck as to what was in each consignment."* Victoria Seymour recalls:*" It was not until the 1950s, when lingering unenthusiastically in front of the shop's window with my ex-Royal Navy, former gunner and radar *operator husband, John, that I began to grasp the significance of the stock within. 'Just look at that', John would say delightedly, pointing to a piece of equipment. 'It's a...' naming it and describing its purpose, while my mind was on what the children were up to. I regret not having paid better attention at the time, never imagining that one day I would want to write about the shop and its owner. I have been aided in this task by the book, 'Stories of the Sea', in which Malcolm told his life story to Jim Coleman."*

Malcolm, a Hastings fisherman, is described in the book as a man whose veins ran not with blood but salt water; the sea was his life and his living. He was born on May 9th 1895; his mother was from an old fishing family, the Wizel Whites, his grandfather one of the first coxswains of the lifeboat. Malcolm attended the ragged school in Tackleway but it's said his real source of education was the sea. He began beachcombing, or as it was known, *"gravel hunting"*, at the age of seven, mostly for wood. Tales of confrontations with the coastguard and details of profitable and strange finds on the beach abound in his early life. When he was twelve he found a half sovereign (55p), which he gave to his mother; on another occasion he pulled from the rocks a half rotten black chamois leather bag containing many more sovereigns. Washed ashore and into his hands were cases of ship's candles, a 140 gallon barrel of port wine, a drum of grease and a sack of flour, which was protected by a skin of paste formed by seawater; it made bread for several families. One find was two little drowned monkeys, joined together by a rope through their collars. A frequent bounty was timber, usually put to use as firewood; one lot in good condition went to the local undertaker to make coffins. Destined by fate to be a life saver, at aged nine Malcolm, along with a friend, rescued two little girls, who fell into the sea where the water and mud were deep. In the First World War Malcolm served on the Minesweeper *HMS Haldon PM5*, which went to rescue of a ship that was blown up by a mine, saving all of the 72 crew except one. A month later, the *Haldon* suffered a similar fate. In peace and wartime he saved or helped to save 169 people on 13 occasions; he held the national record for lifesaving at sea. Malcolm died in 1976; he had retired from auxiliary coastguard duties in 1968, after having served for 34 years. Jim Coleman said in tribute in the foreword to his book: *"You have known what it is to be hungry... your character is always trying to help others...I wish that time will bring a few such as Malcolm Mitchell."* The Mitchell brothers, Tom and Jim, carried on the business until the store closed in 1988 and the entire stock of government and Admiralty surplus was put up for auction, marking the end of an era. Tom, then aged 73, said: *"I joined the business when I was demobbed. I have mixed feelings about packing up the shop but my 81 year-old brother is in poor health so the shop must close."*

Talk to local people in the appropriate age group today and you will find that they or their family bought things at Malcolm Mitchell's store. Brian Lawes, known today as a Hastings writer and historian, remembers in his youth going to Malcolm Mitchell's store. *I bought tank aerials to make into fishing rods and an officer's bridge coat there to wear motorcycling; I still have it."* Colin Smart was 15 when he left school in 1963 to start work with Goodsell, the Hastings builder. There was no special clothing for building site workers then and the men wore either old, everyday clothes or went to stores like Malcolm Mitchell's, to buy war surplus goods. The most important item for heavy or dirty work was a pair of boots and the store stocked these by the ton. Colin said: *"The boots were in huge piles, as if a lorry had turned up and just tipped the whole lot out. A few pairs were tied together by the laces but mostly they weren't and you had to search the pile, until you found two of the same size that were not too worn and seemed to be a pair. To carry my Thermos flask and sandwiches to work I bought an ex-army knapsack; they were very commonly used for this purpose at that time. Later on, I adopted the Mod style of dress and Mitchell's was the place to buy the parka we all wore. I also bought an ex-navy reefer jacket there; it had black buttons on it and I wanted to replace these with metal ones. Mitchell's had buckets full of military buttons and you could search through these until you found a set for the front and the cuffs of the coat. Malcolm would leave you alone to get on with it and when you asked him how much he only charged about a shilling."*

Eric Hughes, a contemporary and friend of Colin Smart, was also a Malcolm Mitchell customer, While Eric was still at school he was bought ex-army, white plimsolls for gym lessons and his first working gear came from the store: *"I started work on road building when I left school and of course, I needed boots. These were at the rear of the shop and cost two shillings a pair, it was like a huge jumble sale, nothing was organised; you could walk right through to the back of the premises. I also bought thick, ex-Royal Navy, roll-necked sweaters and white, sea boot socks. I had a parka from Mitchell's and one of those khaki, peaked knitted caps; you could roll down the brim and tie it under the chin for extra warmth, they were very popular. Malcolm had just about everything ex-war department on sale there, except weapons. For hiking I bought ex-army water bottles but I also remember seeing empty ammunition boxes, which people would use for tools, army and navy blankets, we had these on our beds at home, army greatcoats, ex-navy duffle coats, with wooden toggle fasteners, cap badges, cooking pots, knives, forks, bed sheets and bath towels. You could get almost anything there."*

The public sale of the Mitchell's shop and contents was organised by South East Auctions, of Hastings High Street; managing director and auctioneer Ian Porter said that it took two week's full time working, as well as evenings and weekends, to sort everything into lots. Much of the stock had not been touched since the 1940s and was only discovered in the course of the preparation for the auction. Prospective buyers flocked to find bargains among the mountains of boots, buttons, clothing and cutlery. The 1,300 lots attracted sums varying from £1 to £420, which it was hoped would raise a total of between £15,000 and £20,000. Malcolm Mitchell's store and the premises next door, previously the undertaker Banfield and Pomphrey, were eventually taken over by Paschal McCann and his partner Thierry Zbinden. In the Old Town, rumours abounded about the future use of the shop, at one point conjecture was that it would be a Chinese restaurant and takeaway. The two premises combined opened in August 1998 as the elegant "Interior Illusions", selling unusual gifts and stylish home furnishings. Still trading today, the shop's window displays, particularly at Christmas, are a focal point in the High Street; a far cry from Malcolm Mitchell's mountains of old boots and buckets of buttons.

May 1945

Wartime Hastings had been a vast adventure playground for boys; the local paper all too often featured stories of youngsters who had been injured when playing with illicitly obtained explosives. On 2nd May two local boys, Edward Stevenson, 16 and Ronald Ryves, 14, were admitted to hospital with serious injuries as a result of the explosion of a mine detonator on Ecclesbourne Cliffs. The Observer reported: *"The boys were together on the East Hill when one of them found the detonator. A fire is said to have been started, on which the detonator was placed, the boys suffering in the resulting explosion. They were rushed to the Royal East Sussex Hospital in a serious condition, with injuries and shock. The mine detonator is believed to have been one of more than 50, which were missing after the clearance of a coastal area in the neighbourhood of Fairlight. A search has been made for the others and a warning has been circulated to local schools about the danger of tampering with them. They contain four ounces of high explosive with fuse arrangements, which make them extremely dangerous for inexperienced persons to handle."* Two days later it was reported that the condition of both boys was fairly satisfactory. The authorities asked the Observer to make it known that anyone finding these detonators or having knowledge of where the missing ones were, should not touch them but immediately inform the police.

~~V~~

It was becoming clearer that the announcement of victory was imminent so plans for commemorative and celebratory events, church services, military and civil processions and street parties, were set in motion. It was presumed that Hastings and St Leonards' licensed premises would be well patronised. On behalf of the local Licensed Victuallers Association, Mr H Glenister applied for an hour's extension to public house opening times. The nation waited patiently for the official announcement of victory, not knowing that an international situation was causing a hold-up. The capitulation of Germany to the Allies was announced on 7th May but a technicality in the arrangements made with Russia and America, concerning the timing of announcing the news, was delaying the British people's celebration. However, in anticipation, people poured out into the streets all over the country. In London there were thousands in Whitehall outside Downing Street, waiting for the word, unaware of the diplomatic drama taking place inside Number Ten. When the news of the German surrender arrived the Prime Minister was ready to broadcast; hurried phone calls were made to Marshall Stalin and President Truman, so that the announcements could be made simultaneously, but it was found that previously made arrangements did not allow for the war ending so suddenly and the holiday was not to begin until the Prime Minister had spoken. Winston Churchill at last made his broadcast to the nation: *"Yesterday morning at 2:41 a.m. at Headquarters, General Jodl, the representative of the German High Command, and Grand Admiral Doenitz, the designated head of the German State, signed the act of unconditional surrender of all German land, sea, and air forces in Europe to the Allied Expeditionary Force, and simultaneously to the Soviet High Command...We may allow ourselves a brief period of rejoicing; but let us not forget for a moment the toil and efforts that lie ahead. Japan, with all her treachery and greed, remains unsubdued. The injury she has inflicted on Great Britain, the United States, and other countries, and her detestable cruelties, call for justice and retribution. We must now devote all our strength and resources to the completion of our task, both at home and abroad. Advance, Britannia! Long live the cause of freedom! God save the King!"* (One result of the delay was that Britain's workers would get a two-day break, with 8th and 9th May declared national holidays.)

Immediately following Churchill's speech the country erupted in celebrations; in Hastings the mayor appeared on the town hall balcony and was greeted by a huge crowd and enthusiastic applause. Over the balcony of Hastings Town Hall hung the flags of the chief allies, Britain, America, Russia and France; the Union Jack once again flew from the flag-mast overhead. After a rain shower in the morning the sun reappeared and the crowds enjoyed perfect victory weather. The seafront was thronged with thousands of holiday-makers, who were still promenading late into the evening. Passing cars were decorated with strings of bunting and even buses had multi-coloured streamers attached to the bonnets. Children waved Union Jacks and dogs had emblems of victory tied to their collars. At the Fishmarket a huge crowd of people of all ages gathered under a canopy of flags and bunting and the fishing boats were dressed over all. In the midst of the crowd stood one of John Carter's trucks, with a piano and jazz band aboard; additional music was provided and amplified courtesy of Hornbrooks, a local wireless supply and repair shop. There was street dancing and singing; a large bonfire was lit on the Rock-A-Nore beach and thunder flashes were let off. Joyce Brewer said: *"Oh, what a lovely day it was! My family went to down to the Old Town to join in victory celebrations but I had to continue working on my milk round, so I couldn't join them. My sister told me years later that it was a wonderful feeling to be among a huge crowd of happy people. And we could now look forward to having no more bombs, planes, doodlebugs or blacked-out streets and homes and no more fears. We could live normal lives and catch up on all we had missed during those six years of war."*

A former WWII police officer remembered the victory celebrations causing no trouble: *"I recollect much church bell-ringing, parades and a great many street parties but everything took place in a very orderly manner."* The Hastings Licensed Victuallers Association saw things rather differently. At a post VE Day meeting, association members complained about the wanton breakage and pilfering of drinking glasses, which had disappeared in fives and sixes of dozens: *"The behaviour of some of the younger men and women was disgraceful; they smashed glasses for sheer devilment. There is something wrong with the education in this country when such behaviour exists."* (Only three years previously a woman had been fined £2.00 by Hastings Magistrates Court, with an alternative sentence of 14 days in prison, for walking out of the Kings Head, Ore with beer glass in hand.) During the VE celebrations there were petty criminals who were just as willing to take advantage of the newly declared victory as they were to exploit war conditions: On 8th May there was a theft from the Wheat Sheaf Pub at Bohemia Road. The thief, who it was believed entered the pub via a ground floor window left partly open, stole 200 cigarettes, a bottle of brandy and £30-£40 in notes and £9 in coins, which were in a tankard, hidden in one of the bars. There is no record of anyone being charged with the offence.

~~V~~

Hundreds of local people made their way to London to witness the excitement in the capital. The Daily Mail reported that jubilation and bonfires blazed from Piccadilly to Wapping: *"The pent up spirits of the polyglot throng that was London in wartime burst out and by 11.00pm the capital was ablaze with enthusiasm. Processions formed out of nowhere, disintegrating for no reason, to reform somewhere else. People marched in step, waving flags, arms linked or embracing, down all the great thoroughfares, and from them, in harmony and discord, came song. Rockets* streaked up to the sky and every car that attempted to pass was covered with humanity. They climbed on the roofs and running boards and hammered on the panels. Ships on the river sounded their sirens for two hours. Fire engines clanged and clattered, summoned by false alarms. In the middle of Piccadilly Circus a man stood under the traffic lights playing an accordion while 30 or 40 couples danced on the pavement. Every cornice and lamppost was scaled. Aircraft soared over Buckingham Palace, their navigation lights like coloured stars. The crowd below, convinced that the Royal Family would not appear, still chanted monotonously. 'We want the King.' The police took no steps to check a gaiety that the people had earned. In spite of the pressure of people there was no violence, some were a little drunk but most were intoxicated by victory. London university students formed a mile long procession that traipsed up and down the strand. At New Cross, South East London, near a bomb site, where a few months before 170 were killed in a V2 rocket attack, people danced and sang round a bonfire built amid the debris and ruins. In the early hours of the morning things became somewhat rougher; the university students started tearing down cinema hoardings in Coventry Street and making bonfires of them. For the first time the police had to intervene and move the crowd on. When the bonfires died down most of the West End celebrants set off to walk home or to try and find somewhere to sleep, leaving just a few revellers to continue singing in the streets."

On the Sunday after Victory was declared 10,000 Hastings and St Leonards people gathered at Alexandra Park for a thanksgiving service. The Hastings Mayor took the salute, as a mile-long victory parade, numbering almost 3,500 and representing almost every form of war and home front services, marched past the War Memorial and into the park.

~~V~~

To mark the end the war and to air his fondness for rhetoric, Frederick Goodsell wrote in his editorial: *"Victory has come. The flags are out. A national holiday has been kept and the bells have rung their victory peals... We rejoice at what has been wrought by the valour of our fighting forces and those of our allies. We know full well this is not the end because of the stern task which must be faced in the Far East so our joy and relief must necessarily be restrained...We, in this Premier Cinque Ports Town have nothing to be ashamed of in the way we have lived through our own particular bit of the war. We shall do well to make our reactions to that testing time the model to our reactions to the reconstruction ahead, and then there will be little to fear for the future wellbeing of our beloved town...We salute the men and women of Hastings who have contributed to the Allied victory in Europe."* Perhaps in deliberate congruity, in the adjoining column was a letter from one who had served in the Far East. *"While I was on leave, VE Day was announced and, as I saw the flags and decorations appearing and later, as I watched the celebrations, a bitter dissatisfaction filled my mind. While no one belittles the glorious European victories, I recall many times extracts from letters received from my comrades in Burma. These are Hastings men, Territorials of 231 Battery, Royal Artillery, Woodland Vale Road, St Leonards. The unit was originally comprised of men from Hastings and District. Now, for various reasons only a fraction of the original unit remains. They have been in Burma since the very beginning of the campaign; they have suffered hardships that cannot be fully appreciated, in their long and hard fight across Burma. What is worse, they feel they have been forgotten by the people of Hastings. In their letters and in consultation with Sergeant Tutt, who has recently returned to this country, I am assured that they have received nothing from the people of Hastings since landing in South-East Asia. Being in such a remote and far-off part of the world, truly they must feel they are the "Forgotten Boys" of Hastings. I suggest if the town's people want to celebrate victory they could do no worse than remember the Hastings boys remaining in 231 Battery, the Hastings Battery still on the front line, by organising some means of showing welcome and gratitude which will be effective when they return. J W M Kemsley, Ex-Bdr, 231 Bty R. A. On leave at Hastings."* Ex-Bombardier Kemsley was not alone in his feelings about the neglect of servicemen. A letter published in the national press on VE Day expressed a soldier's disillusionment: *"This time is no better than 1918. I have been discharged from the services for a year and have no pension. Can I get a job? Can I heck! Unable to go back to my own work through disability, I have to have a light job but no one is really interested in an ex-serviceman who has to start life again in a different kind of employment. In December 1944, MPs were sneering at the ex-serviceman who is driven to beg for a living on the streets, "No ex-serviceman need to go on the streets today," said the Minister of Pensions. But I have yet to learn that any provision has since been made for those of us who have served our country and, unable to get a job, see that selling matches is about the only situation presenting itself on the horizon at the moment. A dole of £2 a week does not seem much reward for four years of service. If it was not for my having swallowed my pride and gone cap in hand to seek organised charity, I know that both my wife and I would have been on the streets long* ago. We are indeed just where we were in 1918; no jobs or homes for heroes."

In Hastings, a different type of post-war resentment was simmering, one which *"Vigilant"* chose to highlight, recounting the attitude meet by an officer serving in the Royal Navy Volunteer Reserve and his wife, on returning to Hastings. *"The young couple is feeling bitter about the treatment they have received from some of their fellow citizens. The officer, just released from hospital, and his wife, both hold emergency food ration cards. On presenting them at a Hastings shop his wife was treated with scant courtesy by the assistant and worse, was subjected to a verbal attack by women waiting to be served. They declared loudly that goods should be kept for those who remained in the town and had withstood the bombing. The officer and his wife have endured the Liverpool Blitz and undergone the trials of war in full measure in the various places they have been stationed. They were naturally hurt and disappointed at the sort of welcome they have received in the place of their birth. They deserve our sympathy. People who stayed put in Hastings during the war have no reason to be proud, arrogant or hostile to those who have returned to the town or have arrived as new residents. It is true that some people spent the war in comparative comfort, just by chance, but others, who were sent away, also suffered hardships. Let us have no more comparisons from the thoughtless minority who indulge in mischief making. Stamp it out!"*

The following week's Observer brought a response to *"Vigilant's"* exhortation from somebody signing themselves "Stayed Put": *"With reference to Vigilant's observations regarding returning evacuees: I have heard such remarks but not about those folks who were directed away for work, retired people or those who were told to leave. Rather have the remarks have been about those who, without warning, threw aside jobs, leaving employers and shopkeepers minus staff. Some also left unpaid accounts. I take no credit for remaining in the town, although I have been bombed out twice. The pleasantness of other folk, the consideration and courtesy of shopkeepers and the generally friendly attitude of everyone, more than atoned, to me, for the risk we took from any unwelcome visitations from the air."*

Within two weeks of victory, reality began to bite on the British Home Front when rations were severely cut; food supplies were to be shared with the liberated European countries.

~~V~~

The Observer announced it was experiencing difficulties with restricted space in newspapers: *"Were are trying to be patient with the querulous readers and those who, if an item in which they are interested in is cut or held over, sense some malign influence at work or imagine the editor has grudge against them. I am afraid to say there are still some people who fail to realise that conditions for newspapers, as for most other undertakings, are still very far from normal. Until paper supply becomes easier, the Observer, in common with all other newspapers, will continue to suffer from pressure on space, which often becomes an editorial nightmare. It is no satisfaction to us to be obliged to hold over until a later issue, reports of current events, covered by members of staff or sent in by contributors, whose kind co-operation we value so highly. We earnestly ask for your indulgence and patience in this matter; it is our constant aim to give everyone a fair show but that we cannot hope to satisfy every demand on our very restricted space all the time. The town has grown busier in recent months; there has been a vast increase in local activities of every kind and the VE celebrations have imposed a tremendous extra pressure on our columns."* This point was certainly true of victory parties. Almost every one was reported in full in the Observer, with careful mention of dignitaries present, guests of honour, the names of organisers and entertainers, right down to the sort of celebration gifts for the children. Much space was given to the party photographs, any one of which could have been substituted for another, with the tables and chairs in the middle of the street, rows of grinning children and the backdrop of proud mothers and grandparents; most of the men being away in the forces or at work.

~~V~~

The coalition government set up by Winston Churchill in 1940, to see Britain through the Second World War, came to an end on 23rd May 1945. The Labour Party was anxious to return to business as usual and fight a general election but Churchill was unwilling to dissolve Parliament before the close of the war in the Pacific. However he had little choice when his coalition partners made clear their intentions to go to the country as soon as possible. It would be the first election to be held in Britain for ten years; the population had become more left-inclined during the war years, in which time the position of the Labour Party had changed dramatically. Churchill had given Labour MPs several key ministries within the national government, including the Ministry of Labour to Ernest Bevin and the Home Office to Herbert Morrison. Clement Attlee, the Labour leader, was made Churchill's Deputy Prime Minister. The effect was to give Labour a wealth of experience in office, which was to prove invaluable to the party in the forthcoming election.

June 1945

About 55 street victory parties were held in Hastings and St Leonards. In the weeks leading up to their 2nd June celebrations, the residents of Oakfield, Sandown and School Roads subscribed a total of £28, to fund a party for 150 Ore Village children. There was dancing in the street to Ron Thwaite's Band and the pupils of Miss Mildred Eldridge's Dancing School entertained. Two former prisoners of war, Privates Stace and Gasson were the guests of honour and were presented with cigarettes and matches. Hastings Mayor, Alderman Blackman, attended with the Deputy Mayor, Mrs Farnfield. This was not the only such party in Ore Village. The various streets vied with each other to put on the best show, coping with various difficulties, including the hilly nature of the roads. The party seating was pews, from the corrugated iron church at the bottom of School Road, (now a private residence). The jars on the table were filled with a mixture of garden and wild flowers; the tables set with a miscellany of crockery and cutlery, usually each child brought their own. Although everybody was probably wearing their best for the occasion, it can be seen from the photograph at the end of this chapter that dress looks generally shabby; the young girl, (third right front) is wearing a coat several sizes too large, while a woman, (first left front) looks as if hers is too tight to fasten. The scarf turbans worn by several women were a cheap and popular wartime head covering. There is no obesity. Local resident Mrs Patsy Haste, nee Hodd, can be seen in the front of the photo, second from the right. She recalls: *"My older brother should have been at that party; he was a returned prisoner of war but was ill at the time and not able to go. He had enlisted in the army at aged 16, falsifying his age, and was captured at Dunkirk. The party food seemed wonderful to us, sandwiches, cakes, jellies and lemonade. The war was terrible. I remember running to rescue my little brother, who was playing in the street, as a German plane flew very low, over our rooftops. I knew the pilot could see us so I threw myself over my brother in the gutter. There was no machine-gun fire but the plane dropped a bomb on the corner of Moscow Road."*

~~V~~

Demobilisation of British servicemen began in mid-June, starting with 30,000 per week, to rise to 60,000 by August. Each was kitted out with a set of clothing that was popularly called, 'the demob suit'. On the 15th June a welcome home party for prisoners of war was held by the Red Cross Prisoners of War Committee, who throughout the war had looked after the next-of-kin of prisoners, packed their POW parcels at the centre and organised their club. The party, *"A final happy duty,"* was held at Woolworth's Cafeteria. The Mayor joined in the welcome and after supper there were speeches, entertainment and community signing, led by Mr Joseph Hay.

~~V~~

Leading up to the Whitsun Bank Holiday, five British minesweepers were seen off Hastings, combing the Channel for stray mines and making ready for when merchant vessels and pleasure steamers could plot their own course, without directions from a convoy. On Whit Saturday, 19th May, the outdoor bathing pool at St Leonards was opened for the first time since its closure on 3rd September 1939, after having been occupied by the military and the Civil Defence department during the war. Councillor P J Morren, chairman of the Corporation Entertainments Committee, performed the opening ceremony and the general public was invited to attend as bathers or spectators. The pool was originally opened on 27th May 1933 so the re-opening almost coincided with the 12th anniversary. The three bathing stations, east of Hastings Pier, opposite to the Cinema de Luxe and at West Marina were also opened. Sea floats were once again available and mackintosh bathing allowed at each station, where experienced attendants were in charge. (Macintosh bathing meant changing into bathing wear in the hotel and walking to the beach, often only across the road, wearing a Macintosh, which was then discarded on the beach.)

Repeating the influx of the Easter Holiday, more than 20,000 visitors arrived at Hastings by train, with thousands of others travelling by bus and bicycle. The town enjoyed a very successful and prosperous weekend with fine weather most of the time. As the first of the peacetime holidays it gave encouraging signs that Hastings had lost none of its popularity. A month later saw the return of one of its important sources of revenue, when the first post-war conference was held at the White Rock Pavilion, it was a successful three-day event that marked a significant step in the recovery of the town. The General Workers Congress brought 700 delegates to Hastings for its Biennial Congress of the National Union of the General and Municipal Workers, representing 750,000 employees.

~~V~~

The new poster to advertise Hastings as a desirable holiday resort was printed in the 8th Army News and the forces newspaper *"Union Jack."* The poster depicted a Norman warrior, with the slogan "Hastings and St Leonards are Getting Ready for Your Invasion."

Lt/Cpl Norman wrote to the Observer: *"I was pleased to see Hastings getting a splash in our services paper. North Africa and Salerno have been my invasions points in the past. But for the future I have a hunch I will be one of those third time lucky people and next invade good old Hastings some time in 1945, as my namesakes did in 1066."*

~~V~~

On the question of a shortage of labour in the hotel and catering business, Councillor F S Bouquet, Chairman of the Health and Pleasure Resorts of Great Britain, made a statement to the Observer, following a visit by their deputation to the Ministry of Labour in London. *"The result of our visit was not altogether satisfactory because it only revealed the very bad position with regard to labour generally. We are not likely to get any labour directed here from London; there is not the slightest hope of it. The only chance we have is to secure more labour from our own population, as in future, we are told, labour will not be directed out of town nor will it be directed to such work as hop and fruit picking. People will not be compelled to do these things as they were before. But the labour position is definitely not a happy one and it is likely to remain so for the next six to nine months. The present priorities are hospitals, transport and laundries. Hotels and catering are not considered a priority industry."*

~~V~~

From his hometown of Bath a man wrote to the Observer: *"People returning from a visit to Hastings are spreading tales of acute food shortages there.*

They tell me that while any amount of ice cream can be had, everything else has to be queued for and that there are long queues, even for bread. I am wondering whether the local authorities can do anything to save the situation by an appeal to the Ministry of Food for increased supplies. The bread queues have a very sinister sound." Inquiries by the Observer indicated that in official quarters the food position relating to rationed goods was not actually as serious as had been suggested at a town council meeting, though there was some shortage of fruit and seasonal vegetable supplies. Other newspaper correspondence of the time covered a smoker's apparent vandalism with a cigarette in the cinema, burning four holes in the back of the writer's coat, *"Which surely could not have been an accident,"* the absence of water from public drinking fountains, and a plea from *"One of the Aged"* for a public convenience without steps, *"As the infirm have great difficulty in negotiating them."* At that time most of Hastings and St Leonards public toilets were situated underground and approached by steep stone stairs. They were often presided over by a stern-looking keeper, who had her own glass-fronted cubby-hole. The attendant would emerge from this at busy times, to put the required penny in the lock, enter the toilet cubicle ahead of the customer and give the seat a swipe with a cloth, probably in the hope of a tip.

~~V~~

Returning servicemen brought accounts of the terrible suffering of war victims. A Hastings soldier, Lance Corporal F V Mitchell, Pioneer Corp, sent the Observer a letter enclosing a copy of a grim statement he took from a Polish girl victim of the Nazi horror camp at Belsen, destroyed after the rescue of prisoners. The Observer reported: *"The terrible story that this 22 year-old Polish girl, Lydia Pieprz, told Lance Corporal Mitchell provided further impressive evidence of the need for bringing the Germans responsible for the barbarous and inhuman camps and other atrocities to swift and stern justice. Owing to space restriction we are unable to give the woman's long account fully but any decent person reading her story will agree that the Germans are not fit to be our friends and will agree with non-fraternisation."* The Polish girl's statement, taken at Lingen, Germany in early June, began, *"My name is Lydia but the Nazis knew me as A15680. I shall bear that number tattooed on my left arm to my dying day, as an unpleasant memory of my sufferings at the hands of the Germans. I was born in Danzig of Jewish parents; my father was a journalist and my mother a poet. I left school at 17, when the Germans marched into Poland. In 1941 they rounded up all the Jews in my town and my parents and brother were among those who were put in the gas chamber and killed. I wished then that I could have died with them, for I felt so alone and unhappy."* The remainder of her story described her experiences, first on forced labour in a war factory for 15 hours a day and then in concentration camps.

~~V~~

Hastings man, the late Ivor White, of the Irish Guards, gained first hand insight of the enemy's wartime suffering, when he was sent to join the occupying forces in Germany, sailing out from Dover on HMS Princess Astrid, in 1945. The ship was a Royal Navy-operated landing-craft carrier and one of a fleet of former Belgian cross-channel passenger ships that were requisitioned for war service: *"In the Channel there were still mines floating about, which had broken loose from their moorings and had been missed by the navy minesweepers. There was a moon, and the sea was quite choppy and I remember spending most of the journey on deck, up at the sharp end. Mounted on the forward deck was a powerful searchlight, which was continually scanning the water ahead for any signs of a mine, as we slowly made our way towards Calais. A journey that takes 75 minutes today must have lasted more than four hours that night."* Ivor and his regiment landed safely in Calais docks, to be herded onto a train that had wooden seats and had obviously been used by the Germans for transporting prisoners. In darkness, the train slowly made its way to the ruins of the first town on the German border, Krefeld, where there was a very large military transit camp. Thousands of troops, of all the allied nations, passed through this camp near the Dutch border, many of them going home for the first time since the end of the fighting. Ivor arrived in the city of Cologne, in ruins from the RAF 1,000 bomber raids. The only useable bridge across the Rhine was a pontoon, a floating platform, which swayed as he drove over it. Cologne Cathedral seemed to have escaped the destruction and towered above the devastation. There had been a few feeble attempts by old ladies and children to rescue some of their belongings from the rubble, where hundreds of dead bodies were left. *"There was a distinct smell associated with the Cologne rubble that reminded me of the bombed sites I saw in London after our Blitz. The sight of slightly bedraggled and very polite children following us around, waiting for discarded cigarette stubs soon parted us from our NAAFI ration. Chocolate, cigarettes and tins of corned beef were sometimes traded for souvenirs on the black market, but quite often were just given to children; those whose fathers had either not come home or were in some displaced persons camp, waiting to be identified. I 'volunteered' to become an officer's servant, known as a batman in other regiments and was privileged to live in the commandeered, private house of a local factory owner. It was here that I began to learn German. Among other duties, I was occasionally assigned to the Hamburg Law Courts, as a court room sentry during trials for various cases, varying from those of the major war criminals to the petty offenders charged with stealing coal."* Ivor made many friends while serving in post-war Hamburg. One, who was just a little girl in 1945, used to call at the barracks each day to get a bowl of soup from the field kitchen the occupying forces set up outside the barrack gates. She carried her young brother in her arms, so that they would be allowed two helpings. Then they would go home to share the soup with their mother. In 1999, this child saw an article about Ivor's Irish Guards' website in a German newspaper and contacted him and they corresponded with him for years.

The School Road, Ore Village, victory party, June 1945

Middle Street victory party held on the bomb site in Havelock Road

Crowds at Hastings Fishmarket celebrate the announcement of Victory in Europe

Hastings Town Centre mid-1940s; note two major bomb sites, the Albany Hotel and Havelock Road

Part of the tanks that held the fuel for the flames defence system

The "Reluctant Air Raid Shelter" in Caves Road

One way of getting rid of wartime defence installations

Malcolm Mitchell, fisherman and proprietor of the Old Town government surplus store

July 1945

Hastings was given welcome publicity on the BBC by the popular broadcaster Miss Jean Metcalfe. In his column, *"Vigilant"* expressed his gratitude to her for having done the town a good service. As well as playing record requests in her radio programme, *"Two Way Family Favourites"*, Miss Metcalfe read out the letters accompanying the requests from men serving overseas. The piece she broadcast about Hastings was reproduced in the Observer: *"I was reading some of your letters while on a train the other day and I came across one from Italy, it was yours Fred, and in it you told me about a little blue lagoon you had discovered at Sorrento. Reading about that little beach, as I sat in a train was like a real endurance test; the weather here was the nearest thing to a heat wave we have had this summer. And then, right on cue, I looked out the window at a poster on Purley Station. It was one of the finest I'd seen for ages; a brightly coloured, 1066 soldier, sitting on a cliff-top. The caption read, 'Hastings is Getting Ready for Your Invasion.' I set out for Hastings for the day. It did not take more than a few minutes to walk from the station to the Albert Memorial, where the flower beds, brimming with marigolds and geraniums, dispelled all ideas of the dilapidation I had expected to find after five years of Hastings being a front line town. There are still signs up saying 'First Aid Post' and 'Ungassed Citizens This Way,' at the entrance to the underground car park that runs under the promenade; just to remind you that not long ago the car park was an air raid shelter. There still are quite few ragged gaps in the rows of hotels and boarding houses, showing that not all the German bombs fell in the sea. But for the most part, Hastings has put its house back in order and crowds of people were on the beach and along the promenade, the deck chair men were doing a roaring trade and the sea was dotted with brightly-coloured rafts. The rock plants were in full bloom in the White Rock Gardens and the White Rock Pavilion was leading a double life, as the ration book distribution centre, as well as the home of the Clarkson Rose seasonal revue 'Twinkle.' At the other end of the promenade, towards the East Cliff, the whelk and cockle stalls couldn't have been busier, even on a bank holiday. I hopped on a bus to have a look at Hastings Castle; it was a pleasant surprise to find there are still penny bus tickets in this part of the world. On the cliff-top a small boy, aged about three or four, was flying a kite, probably for the first time since the ban was lifted and, I suppose, for* the first time in his life. Looking at the sea below, I saw a brown-sailed fishing boat just coming ashore. After queuing at home and in London for dubious looking fish, this was too good an opportunity to miss. I lost no time in climbing down the cliff path and arrived just in time to see the fish spread out on the flagstones. I wandered round the streets of the old town, which never seems to change. If you have spent holidays at Hastings you are bound to remember the rows of tarred, wooden sheds, where the fishing nets are stored. The wood of these tall narrow sheds is old and blistered and they lean against each other like books on a shelf. An old fisherman, smoking a clay pipe and with rings in his ears, was working by one the sheds and he told me that fishing nets, like silk stockings, have to repaired to the last thread because they can't be replaced these days. The fishermen's church is still there but it was undergoing repairs so I could not look in to see if the walls were still hung with nets, as they used to be. But I expect that like most other things I saw, it's unchanged. This piece of Sussex coast may not be as artistic as the one you told me about in Sorrento, Fred, but the people I saw at Hastings, taking their first seaside holiday for years, seemed to be very satisfied. As I am sure you will be too, when you get back home. Till then, Sorrento sounds like a very good substitute to me, and I daresay this song will always have happy associations for any of you of Combined Military Forces who have spent your leave there."* It is not known if Fred was a Hastings man or the name of the song he chose, but it surely can only have been "Back to Sorrento", a Neapolitan song that became wildly popular after the war, due to its being frequently played in gramophone request radio programmes.

~~V~~

The 5th July 1945 was General Election Day. After strenuous campaigning and some lively public meetings, polling in Hastings proceeded quietly. The three candidates: Major F. M Cooper-Key (Conservative), Captain Lewis Gassman (Labour) and Mr S M Parkman JP (Independent Progressive) toured the borough. Confidence in the results was expressed by all the political camps and there was, *"No lack of cheerfulness in the party offices."* The weather for polling day was fine and sunny and the townspeople turned out to vote in great numbers, estimated to be two thirds of the electorate. However, the veteran Conservative agent, Mr R F Boutwood, for whom this was his tenth fight, would only go as far as to describe it as a very heavy poll. In 1945 there was a total of 36,181 voters on the electoral roll, including 3,574 military service voters. Polling stations opened at 7.00am and after a slow trickle for the first two hours there was a steady stream of voters throughout the day. The first to arrive, at 7.01am, at Mount Pleasant were a husband and wife. Blind people, who voted in considerable numbers, were among the earliest to turn out. The youngest on the electoral register was Valerie P Monk, aged three, of 41, Emmanuel Road, who of course, was not allowed to vote. At West St Leonards, where the poll was close to 100%, a woman was not allowed to vote because it was her ten-year-old daughter's name on the list. There was a three-week delay before the final result could be announced because the postal votes of service personnel had to be gathered. On Thursday 26th July at 9.00am the Conservative candidate, Major Cooper-Key (Conservative) was declared victorious with a total vote of 14,105 votes and a majority of 3597. Captain Gassman (Labour) attained 10,508 votes and Mr Parkman (Independent Progressive) 2564; he forfeited his deposit of £150, failing to poll at least one eighth of the total cast. From outside the White Rock Pavilion, where the count had taken place in the lower hall with the help of 40 clerks, Cooper-Key said, *"This election result is a message of confidence in our Lord Warden* [Churchill] *from the Premier Cinque Port.* [Hastings]*"*

Clement Attlee was elected Britain's new Prime Minister after Labour won a sweeping victory. The outgoing Prime Minister and great wartime leader, Winston Churchill, immediately went to Buckingham Palace to tender his resignation; Mr Attlee was welcomed by the King shortly afterwards and asked to form a new Government. Mr Attlee promised a new order and an economic policy to raise the standards of life for people all over the world. In a resignation statement Mr Churchill expressed, *"Profound gratitude for the unflinching and unswerving support given to me by the people of Britain during the war years."* Labour's landslide victory came as a major shock to the Conservatives. During the election campaign Mr Churchill had appealed to the country to give his new National Government, formed after the dissolution of the Coalition government in May, a good majority. But his appeal was rejected, largely, it is thought, because Britain believed Labour's promises to implement the Beveridge Report. Thus Attlee's 1945 victory marked a watershed in British history and ushered in the Welfare State and the National Health Service.

After the General Election, Hastings Watch Committee proposed to ban the use of loudspeakers on cars for advertising and other purposes and suggested that they should be used by the police only, in cases of grave emergency. *"Vigilant"* agreed, commenting in his column: *"Very few people will quarrel with this and most will hope that the appropriate by-law will be introduced as soon as possible. A London magistrate, dealing with a case of nuisance caused by election loudspeakers said, 'A nuisance is nuisance, whether it is advertising pills or a political candidate.' The recent General Election campaign provided plenty of evidence of the loudspeaker menace. It was too much to hope that the parties locally would have stood out against this doubtful aid to their campaigning. Although I heard many noises, as the candidates' amplifiers toured the streets, I failed to extract any connected arguments that would have influenced my voting."*

~~V~~

On the Thursday 6th May 2010, voters went to the polls in the most tightly-contested General Election in a generation. Polling stations opened at 7am and closed at 10.00pm. There was greater uncertainty about who would emerge as Prime Minister than in any election since 1992 and the real expectation of a hung parliament for the first time since 1974. Much depended on the parties' performance in individual constituencies, particularly the 100 or so Labour/Conservative marginals, Hastings being one of these. Since 1945 there had been a number of boundary changes and the constituency, now known as Hastings and Rye, had an electoral roll in the region of 90,000. The candidates were, Michael Foster, (Labour), Amber Rudd, (Conservative), Nick Perry, (Liberal Democrat), Nick Prince, (British National Party), Ron Bridger, (English Democrats) and Tony Smith, (UK Independence Party.) As on the July 1945 Election Day it was fine and sunny on 6th May 2010 in the Hastings and Rye Constituency and polling stations experienced a steady stream of keen voters from the start, one man in Ore arriving ten minutes before the 7.00am opening. The count, which took place in Horntye Sports Centre, built on the site of the former Summerfield School, put Conservative Amber Rudd in power, with 20,461 votes, (majority 1,993). Coming second with 18,475 votes was Michael Foster, a much respected local man, whose vote may have suffered as a result of the unpopularity of the Labour Prime Minister, Gordon Brown. Nick Perry polled 7,825 votes, Tony Smith, 1,397, Nick Prince 1,310 and Rod Bridger 339. There was a 64% turnout. Nationally, the final voting figures were less decisive than in Hastings, resulting in the predicted hung parliament and the expectation of a coalition government. Initial behind-the-scenes negotiations between the three main parties had already begun by afternoon of 7th May.

Saturday 8th May 2010 was the 65th anniversary of VE Day. In the strained political atmosphere generated by the inconclusive outcome of the General Election, the leaders of the three main political parties took time off from talks to attend a ceremony at the Cenotaph, joining Prince Charles, the Duchess of Cornwall, war veterans, serving soldiers, sailors and airmen and 2000 members of the public. Prince Charles and military chiefs laid wreaths, as did each of the party leaders. A minute's silence was observed and a bugler sounded the last post as a tribute to the 580,406 UK and commonwealth forces killed in the six year conflict and the 67,073 civilians who died in the Blitz. A reading from the diary of Winifred Vere Hodgson (1901-1979), described the *"glorious day"* of 8th May, 65 years ago. Laura Crooks, the granddaughter of the WWII veteran Norman Bowie, 89, also present, read the excerpt, which told how crowds celebrated VE Day in London. At the conclusion of the half-hour service, the party leaders left the Cenotaph to resume the political bargaining. A tense three days ensued and it was not until the late afternoon of Tuesday 11th May that the Conservatives completed a deal with the Liberal Democrats, the coalition having Conservative David Cameron as its Prime Minister and Liberal Democrat Nick Clegg as deputy, with members of both parties promised seats in the cabinet. Finally, the traditional post-election visits to Buckingham Place were made by the departing Gordon Brown and the incoming Cameron, at 43 the youngest Prime Minister in 200 years. Political pundits variously predicted that the coalition government, the first in 70 years, could either shape the style of politics for a generation to come or collapse under cross-party tensions.

~~V~~

The Saturday following the 1945 General Election the Observer published details of a captured German aerial photograph of Hastings, seized in Belgium, along with maps and other material, indicating that the town would be one of the enemy's invasion points after the fall of France in 1940. The details on the map indicated the thorough nature of the preparations made by the Germans. The photograph was taken some time before the outbreak of war, for it showed the piers unbreached and the Fishmarket boating lake full of water. The photograph may have been taken from the airship Graf Zeppelin, when it cruised along the Channel in pre-war days, the direction of the shadows suggesting it was mid-morning. The date August 1940 was written in red on the side of the photograph and perhaps more significant was the date 28/8/39 and the German word for agenda. It is believed the information was brought up to date several days before the German invasion of Poland, which led to Britain's declaration of war on 3rd September. The photo covered the central area of Hastings, from the seafront to Silverhill, Ore and Clive Vale. It extended from the Marina, St Leonards, to the Fishmarket, where the harbour and fishing boats, drawn up on the beach, could be clearly seen. There were detailed Ordnance Survey references that would have been of help to the invader if they had secured local maps. So circumspect were the Germans they included the magnetic variation, latitude and longitude and the rise and fall of the tide. A comment in German noted *"rail connection not at hand,"* something the enemy probably regarded as indicating the British lack of efficiency. Other notes expressed doubts about the harbour and mentioned that the piers had buildings for passenger traffic. The German geography was at fault in one important particular. The sea off Hastings was named as Strait of Dover. The shores of Hastings are, in fact, lapped by the English Channel, which proved to be, in spite of German preparation, an impossible barrier and a highway for the Allied invasion.

~~V~~

Hastings returned to full peace-time public lighting on the evening of 15th July, when 3,000 street lamps were switched on. There could have been more lights but the town had lost 145 lamp standards or brackets through enemy action and it was not possible to replace them at the time. The switch-on followed the ending of double summer time, which had given light evenings until 11.00pm. Mr A J Ryan, the retiring Borough Electrical Engineer, said: *"If the Ministry of Fuel and Power decides afterwards to tell us that we must conserve fuel by reducing our street lighting, we shall have to accept their decision. It will not be our fault if we have to curtail the lighting."* It was hoped the restored street lights would encourage more people to come out in the evening and that meetings and entertainments would start at a later hour. The Observer reported a week later that after six years of coastal darkness, the long lines of brilliant lamps on the seafront made a dazzling scene, which drew holiday makers and residents for a late stroll. Young children, who had never seen the streets lit, were amazed and delighted. However, according to the correspondence to the Observer, some of the residents were less so: *"We have been urged in the press and on the radio to save fuel and warned that there may be a serious shortage of coal in the coming winter. The corporation is now wasting fuel every day by lighting the street lamps in the day-time and when there is a good moon. Private individuals are prosecuted when they waste light; is the corporation beyond the law? Exasperated"* The Observer Editor noted that it was understood that labour shortage made it necessary for lamplighters to start early to cover all roads before dusk.

The joy at the end of war in Europe was not universal; a soldier on leave in Hastings felt so troubled by an incident in the Ritz Cinema that he was moved to write a long letter to the Observer. In summary it ran: *"The organist at the Ritz put some words on the screen for us to sing and these upset me. To quote a few of the phrases used: 'It's all said and done, it's all over. No more conscription and munitions. Vera Lynn will soon be Sweetheart of the Boys Brigade.' I think Vera is still Sweetheart of the Forces and will be until it IS all over and done. I've been in the army since 1939 and I have just done three years overseas. I will not now be sent to the Far East and I have no axe to grind for the blokes out there. I just want to say that overseas we were very happy when we knew that the V1 and V2 rockets were finished, it meant that our families were safe. But on VE Day, where I was in Italy, when the unit canteens were being drunk dry to celebrate victory, I don't think many people forgot to lift a glass to the poor ***s out east. They were, and are, still fighting bloody battles for the right to celebrate. I have only been in England for three weeks but it seems to me the tendency to forget these lads is very general. Please don't encourage it by putting up silly stuff in your places of entertainment. Just keep on with War Savings, Comfort Funds and Red Cross support and don't forget, in your time of safety, the men for whom it is not over and done just yet. Pegasus"*

August 1945

Hastings and St Leonards' recovery as a holiday resort was assured when August Bank Holiday brought 40,000 visitors by train and hundreds more by road; the town experienced its biggest August visitor numbers since 1939. All accommodation was fully booked and some people slept out on the Saturday night in shelters at the Marina Bathing Pool. A welcome indication of progress towards financial recovery came with the official figure of £150,000 being spent each week during the peak period. It was reckoned at the time that hotel and guesthouse residents spent on an average of eight pounds per person per week and day-trippers a pound each. A local bank official said that one of the reasons for the high expenditure was the increased prices of accommodation, restaurants, shops and entertainments. To cope with the heavy holiday road-traffic the special constables were called in to assist the regular police. A sight not seen for six years was the hundreds of cars and scores of long-distance coaches parked near the front and in the re-opened underground car parks. At night the seafront was thronged by strolling holiday-makers; others enjoyed the fair at the Fishmarket. Except for two brief showers on the Bank Holiday Monday afternoon, Hastings enjoyed excellent weather through the weekend. Alexandra Park was a popular destination and crowds admired the best floral display seen there in years. The beaches were packed and there were long queues at restaurants and ice cream shops. Shortages of all kinds of goods were still apparent and *"Vigilant"* had something to say about this, with reference to cigarettes and alcohol: *"It is a disgrace that there are visitors who come to Hastings and St Leonards for the sole purpose of going from shop to shop, until all the tobacconists and licensed premises are sold out."* Alcohol was generally in short supply and people would go to considerable lengths to buy and sell it, as the following court case reveals. Saucily headlined, *"The Waitress and the Whisky"* the Observer's Magistrates' Courts report ran: *"A café waitress gave evidence in Hastings Magistrates Court that she had paid a man £2 for what she thought was a bottle of whisky, but when she examined the bottle later she found the word 'Dummy' visible on the bottle. A police witness had tasted the contents and said that it was possibly tea. Before the court was Joseph Brady, who was remanded in custody for a week on the application of Superintendent Knell, on a charge of stealing £2 by a trick. Mrs Cecilia Simmins, a waitress at her sister's café at 10 George Street, said that Brady brought the bottle in a sack containing 70 pounds of peas, which her sister agreed to buy. When Brady opened the sack in the kitchen to empty out the peas he put the bottle on the table; it was properly sealed. She asked him if he wanted to sell it and he told her she could have it, saying, 'Give me two pounds and a shilling to buy myself a drink with.' Mrs Simmons gave him the money and also paid him one pound on account for the peas, at sixpence a pound. Brady said he would return for the balance of 15 shillings. After he had gone Mrs Simmons held the bottle up to the light and saw the word 'Dummy.' PC Jupp said that when Brady was charged he said. 'She only gave me 30 shillings.' Sergeant Pike Brady stated the accused said that he had brought the bottle from a soldier in a public house."*

~~V~~

Six naval ratings and two officers from the sloop, *HMS Hastings,* adopted by the town after Warship Week, came as the guests of the town corporation, from Friday night until Tuesday morning. They were given a civic reception at the town hall and enjoyed the freedom of the borough, visited entertainments and sporting events and were given a warm welcome everywhere. During the war, *HMS Hastings* had been on East Coast convoy work. The crew claimed she was one of the first ships to be bombed, on the Moray Firth in 1939; she was also machine-gunned by enemy planes. During one of these attacks, a crew member was wounded and was later awarded the Conspicuous Gallantry Medal.

~~V~~

Resorting to a form of strong language that was rarely seen it print at the time, the town council said that they were, *"doing their damnedest"* in their efforts to ease the housing crisis in Hastings. The Housing Committee was determined to use to the full its powers of requisitioning empty dwellings for immediate use. They set up a Committee of Action of four members, to meet daily, in order to speed up the housing drive. A report received from the borough treasurer showed that in September 1944 there were 4,208 houses and flats empty, but nearly 1,900 of these properties had since become occupied. The effects of the *'speeding up'* began to show immediately; five houses for sale, which had been empty for some time in Queens Road near the railway bridge, bore requisition notices on their doors. A number of other empty houses in various parts of the town were also requisitioned or under consideration. The property owners had 14-day right of appeal to the local authority.

~~V~~

In the hey-day of British seaside resorts, the public shelters of the sun trap variety were of much more significance than today, when they serve mainly as bus shelters. Many boarding houses had strict rules about guests vacating their lodgings after breakfast and not returning until the evening meal. If the weather was wet, the holiday-makers found almost no free indoor places to spend time, so, to the hard up, the shelters were much in demand, to eat fish and chips or just sit down out of the rain. Along with public toilets, the standard of the shelters was regarded as a hall-mark of a good holiday destination. So it was not surprising when *"Vigilant"* turned his attention to them, after an Observer reader had written to the paper about the disgraceful state of the shelter at Demark Place. This specimen could have been described as a palace among Hastings shelters; it was the size of a large room and furnished with wooden benches. The shelter was situated close to Woolworths and the Carlisle Pub and stood above one of Hastings' largest subterranean public toilets, which probably pre-dated the shelter. By the early 1950s it was fully glazed with doors that shut out the gales. What matter that the smell of disinfectant rose up from the toilets below, flavouring the holiday-makers' picnics? On the matter of the vandalism of the shelter Vigilant wrote: *"I have confirmed that the shelter at Denmark Place is in a truly deplorable state and it demands an immediate clean up. Its walls are crying out for a coat of whitewash, expedient in the interests of decency; it also needs regular sweeping. Later, the walls must be treated to make a repetition of the present defacement impossible. Other shelters like this are rendered ineffective through lack of glass and it is hoped these will be put right soon. But the Denmark Place chamber of horrors must be dealt with at once."* The Denmark Place shelter was eventually demolished in a rash of town improvements, the toilets beneath filled in and the ground concreted over, providing an outdoor drinking and smoking spot for the Carlisle Pub customers. Vandalism was not limited to buildings; in a letter that resonates all too keenly with present correspondence to newspapers; an Observer reader adopted a sarcastic tone: *"Wanted: More fencing to break up, more trees to break down, more bottles to smash, more seating to break up. What a pity the children and youths do not appreciate the efforts that were made to acquire the playground at Red Lake. No one seems to care about its maintenance except for the occasional cutting of the grass. Who is responsible for its care? Does the road sweeper ever go there? Do the police ever bother to look in? No. Seats may be smashed up, trees and fencing broken and removed, swings taken down. No one ever bothers who did it or where they are. Parents and children should see that the gifts of playgrounds are looked after and not abused. Why not hand the ground over to the Parks and Garden Committee to look after with the same care as the bowling greens? Put down a good surface of tar macadam for the lower part, not tarred ashes as at present and give the police instructions to supervise the playground."*

~~V~~

On the 8th and 9th of August, the dropping of atomic bombs on Hiroshima and Nagasaki brought about the end of the war with Japan. These two cities were almost totally destroyed, with immense loss of life. Japan surrendered on the 14th August and the Allied Forces were ordered to suspend hostilities immediately. In Hastings there were not the immediate scenes of public joy that had occurred at the announcement of the ending of the war in Europe; many people were at work when the news came through. The Observer said that there were no excited scenes but the news of victory was received in the town in a spirit thankfulness that the six years of war were finally over. A special meeting of the Entertainments Committee was called and immediate arrangements were made for a two-day celebration. It was decided that the White Rock Pavilion should be thrown open to the public for dancing on each holiday night from 8.00pm to 2.00am and that the Bathing Pool should open free-of-charge at the same time. Housewives, taking no chances over food supplies, were out shopping straight after breakfast and there were queues at nearly every food shop. Some of the town's leading eating-out places were closed, resulting in long queues at those that remained open. After dark, many residents on the seafront adopted a suggestion that they should leave their curtains open, to add to the illuminations; several houses had special light displays. Large crowds of residents and visitors took part in the celebrations at Alexandra Park, the West Hill and the Bathing Pool. Predictably, the best fun was to be had in the Old Town, where singing, street dancing, wild behaviour, thunder flashes and bonfires took over. The riding lights of the fishing boats on the beach were reported, *"A pretty picture."* Lady Rosemary Spencer Churchill and the Duchess of Marlborough mingled almost unnoticed in the midst of the revellers." A soldier was seen standing on the platform of a bus, playing the bagpipes, regardless of the boarding and alighting passengers and the Queen Victoria statue in Warrior Square was decorated with a beach sign that declared, 'Bathing Now Prohibited.' Many public houses ran out of beer and put up notices saying, *"Closed until further supplies arrive."* One popular hostelry announced to its customers. *"Open at 8.30pm. Remnant Sale";* while another offered, *"Peace and goodwill to all men, but no beer."*

If there was any idea that London had been satiated with VE Day celebrations in May the following account from the Daily Mail dispels it: *"London went crazy last night. Despite the hints early yesterday that it had been caught on the wrong foot again, the rollicking thousands who turned out to celebrate made the biggest and noisiest crowd London ever saw. Never before has Piccadilly staged such scenes. I tried to write this story in a telephone kiosk just off Piccadilly; it was impossible. Outside the mob rocked and swayed and marched, banging at the windows of the kiosk, shouting, cheering, dancing and singing, climbing up lamp-posts; just going crazy with peace. For two hours I fought to get to Eros, from a starting point at Great Windmill Street. Eventually, I gave up. The police told me, 'Nobody could get through that crowd.' The dancing crowds performed everything from the 'Can-Can' to 'Knees up Mother Brown.' Hundreds of fireworks; Catherine Wheels, rockets, squibs and jumping crackers, went off every minute. The whole sky above Piccadilly blazed with rockets and fireworks, lighting up the faces of the shrieking, laughing crowds. The Red Cross emergency stations around Piccadilly continually received fresh cases from the crowd; women who had fainted, men who had been knocked over and trampled on, sprained ankles, broken wrists. Girls were being thrown into the air by jubilant men only to fall many feet away into the crowd. Some were hurt. In the few public houses still open late at night the occupants were prisoners, as they could not get out due to the pressure of crowds in the street, while the thirsty ones fought for hours trying to get in. Street hawkers were still doing business; flags fetching from one shilling (5p) to seven shilling and sixpence (38p) and victory rattles five shillings (25p). Thousands slept out in London last night. They had to, for the midnight queues for trains, trams and buses were far too long for all to get home. Main line stations, air raid shelters, the parks and even shop doorways were packed with sleepers.*

Sunday 15th August 2010 marked the 65th anniversary of Victory over Japan: a commemorative ceremony and service took place at the Cenotaph in London. Present were Prince Charles, the Duchess of Cornwall, Prime Minister David Cameron, representatives of the three military services, veterans of the conflict and members of the public, The ceremony was organised by the Ministry of Defence and Burma Star Association. Services were also held around the UK, honouring the loss of almost 30,000 UK lives in the Far East. The Cenotaph service began with prayers, followed by the Last Post sounded by the Buglers of the Band of Her Majesty's Royal Marines, Commando Training Centre Royal Marines. Viscount John Slim, President of the Burma Star Association, read the Kohima Epitaph: *"When you go home, tell them of us and say, for your tomorrow, we gave our day."* Of the hundreds of thousands who fought, 12,500 died in Japanese prison camps. Speaking ahead of the Cenotaph service, Prime Minister David Cameron said: *"We must never forget the sacrifices made and the dedication showed by those who served our country in the Second World War. They lost their lives and many were imprisoned. And they did all this for us, to protect the freedoms we all enjoy today. VJ Day, the day the Second World War ended, is a time for this generation to reflect and show its gratitude to our veterans for their bravery, dedication and sacrifice."*

September 1945

Hastings Trades Councils protested about a statement by the Borough Engineer Sidney Little, in which he had made an unfavourable comparison between the work output of the German prisoners of war and British labourers on local house-building sites; Little declined to withdraw his statement, saying that the Germans' work was fifty percent better. The Trades Council viewed this further statement as provocative and anti-social and once again invited Little to withdraw his statements. He refused. In defence of local building workers Councillor Riddle said: *"I recently attended a Trades Council where 60 members said that the British building trade operatives working on the Rocks Lane scheme were in the main old men, suffering from physical defects and unable to run up ladders and across roofs. They cannot be compared to Germans, who have been trained for a war and are in the prime of life. The Germans also have the additional incentives in the way of extra rations, if they work well. To compare the diluted, local labour force available in Hastings with the German workers is grossly unfair and misrepresents the whole situation. Things will change on the building sites when our own workers are demobilised from the forces."* Councillor Stephenson said that had Germany won the war, our men would have been working in Germany and would have been driven by the whip. Predictably, the letters to the Hastings Observer were many, some correspondents supporting Little's views. One saying: *"Contrary to popular belief, the Germans do not have extra rations and, additionally, work longer hours.* The expectation that the return of men from the services would speed up house construction was not realised on the Rocks Lane building site. By autumn 1947 progress was slow, due to a shortage of labour; during the previous summer work had been delayed by a union dispute.

The War Department announced on November 21st 1945 that thousands of German prisoners of war would be handed over to European governments for labour battalions to help rebuild liberated Europe. In 1946, more than 400,000 German POWs were still being held in Britain, mainly in camps on the outskirts of towns. The POWs were important to the Britain's economy; there were still one and three quarter million of her own men in the services. At one point post-war, one in five manual workers was a POW. They were doing up to one fifth of all farm work in Britain and were also employed on road works and building sites. Fraternisation between the soldiers and the local population was strictly forbidden but the ban was lifted in time for Christmas 1946. In towns across Britain, many people chose to put the war behind them and invite German POWs to join them for a family Christmas; the first the men had experienced in years. By the end of 1947, around 250,000 German POWs had been repatriated, but 24,000 decided to stay in Britain. In 1948 POWs worked on Wembley Stadium in preparation for the London Olympic Games. The last German POWs were repatriated in November 1948.

~~V~~

The president of Hastings Rotary Club, Thomas Crump, thanked local people for their support in providing clothing for the people of Holland, while making one final appeal via the Observer, saying that many more parcels were needed. Baling and forwarding of the clothing was to begin on Monday 10th September. Mr Crump said: *"Please have another look through your wardrobes and see what you can spare. With cold and wintry weather drawing nearer the need is getting urgent. Our treasurer will be pleased to arrange the collection of parcels if getting them to our depot is difficult."* The people of Hastings had already donated over 5000 items of clothing and footwear to the scheme. Others had sent money to help with running expenses; the Rotary Club said that any cash left over would be forwarded to the Netherlands Red Cross. This generosity from Hastings to the Netherlands and other European countries continued for some time. It was noted in their minutes that in 1946 the Unitarian Church, where Emile Crane and her Lavender Cottage friends worshipped, the Ladies' Society had sent parcels of clothing to the Netherlands, as well as doing what they could to support refugees.

Earlier in 1945, an appeal had been made for second-hand fabrics to be donated to help the war-stricken countries of Europe, although dressmaking and household textiles were still rationed and in short supply for the citizens of Great Britain. If proof were needed of this it was when blackout curtains were finally discarded. There was an outbreak of home made dirndl skirts and aprons, the black fabric relieved with rows of colourful rick-rack braid or embroidery. Dr Ethel Lee, the County Organiser of the Women's Voluntary Service, unwisely delayed an appeal for blackout curtains to be sent to France to make pinafores for girls and boys, as this was standard dress at the time for both sexes. After years of experience the home dressmaker had become highly skilled at making the best of whatever materials she could get. In early September, Mrs Burton of 60, Fairlight Road, Ore, won the first prize of ten pounds in a national competition in make-do-and-mend, set by the Board of Trade. The winning item was described as: *"A charming and colourful housecoat, made in sparkling patchwork, which cost only one shilling in outlay: The materials used were a discarded bed tick (mattress cover), a shirt, the remains of an old dance dress, trimming off an old dress and patchwork pieces from scrap bags, given to Mrs Burton by her friends. Also used were embroidery silks left over from fancy needlework, and the buttons, bias binding, shoulder pads and cord from an old wedding dress."*

~~V~~

On 13th September Hastings Mayoress, Mrs Blackman, went for lunch aboard *HMS Hastings,* which was paying an official visit. Mrs Blackman was accompanied by Major W H Dyer, the Borough Publicity Officer, as the mayor, her father-in-law, was too ill to be present. Calm and sunny conditions prevailed when the ship anchored two miles off the town; many local boats went out to cruise round it. But rough weather sprung up during Thursday afternoon, after the official lunch, and Mrs Blackman was marooned. Two attempts were made to bring the mayoress ashore by Hastings lifeboat, but the seas were running so high it was only possible to ferry the officers and ratings. Major Dyer was able to jump from the ship to the lifeboat but it was considered was far too risky for the mayoress to attempt it, as the sea was lifting the gangway up and down five feet. Officers and ratings who had gone ashore to attend a dance at the White Rock Pavilion were unable to return their ship, so were accommodated at the theatre, sleeping on settees, under blankets provided by Hastings Sea Cadets. The officers stayed at the Dorland Hotel where the officers and ratings had early morning tea, going out for breakfast.

On Friday evening, when *HMS Hastings* was almost obscured from sight, due to sheets of rain being driven by gales, it was decided the mayoress should remain aboard, to be disembarked at a naval port, possibly Portsmouth, thus curtailing the official visit. There was no concern for Mrs Blackman's safety, a message from the ship said; *"She is quite well and comfortable and enjoying her novel experience."* The storm abated and after a short trip across still choppy seas; Mrs Blackman finally stepped ashore at Hastings Pier on Saturday morning, she said she had enjoyed her stay on the ship and had been marvellously treated and had not been seasick, The vessel steamed away on Monday morning. In October, the Mayor presented the ship with an engraved, silver cigarette casket, to commemorate the historic visit of HMS Hastings to her namesake town.

~~V~~

Vigilant turned his disapproval on what he called *"Queuing Mania,"* agreeing with the Chairman of the Food Control Committee, Mr Percy Idle, that there are people who will queue for anything, anywhere, at any time: *"A sheep-like section of the public is quite prepared to line up for non-essentials and one wonders how long this queue mentality, once established, will last. The fact that they might miss something that is going, subjects those queuing to hours of inconvenience and boredom, for the sake of an ice-cream or a few biscuits, which they could get without any trouble at all if they were content to bide their time. It is up to the more intelligent of the public to resist these manifestations of the herd instinct, or the return to normal living will be greatly delayed if not made quite impossible."* He then focused his attention to the matter of bus stop queues, saying that he would not be so foolish as to suggest all queues could be avoided and that he believed much waiting was caused by shortage of labour. But bus queues could be shortened if young people were not too lazy to walk short distances: *"Waiting in a queue of nearly 100 people for bus to an outlying part of the borough this week, I was disgusted to see the number of young children lined up in the rush hour. On the top deck of the bus that I eventually boarded there were no fewer than ten children, who, in my opinion, ought not to have been allowed on the bus at all at that time of day. But as our bus company shows no sign of considering the town's workers, by issuing priority tickets or adopting any device to give long distance travellers a fair chance against those who are only going a short distance, it seems the townspeople must grin and bear it. They must also learn to have patience with the vagaries of the conductors, who cannot decide how many passengers are to stand in their buses. I understand the Board of Trade regulations state the number eight. But this can be five or even none at all, as the conductor of a bus on the circular route, at a crowded bus stop at the Memorial on Tuesday, seemed to think."*

~~V~~

A lengthy discussion was held at a town Council meeting on the subject of the new promenade tea trolley, on display at the meeting, complete with an attendant. The green and cream trolley, topped with a tea urn and trays for cakes below, stood in the corner of the room during a meeting of the Entertainments Committee. The committee took a break and treated members of the council, the local press and themselves, to a good cup of tea. Councillor P J Morren handed round the tea in cream and green cups, emblazoned with the borough arms; cakes of all kinds followed. The urn-made tea was considered to be very good, with no suggestion of it being over-brewed. The catering manager, Mr H G Nightingall explained: *"The urns are thermostatic and the tea made three hours previously and should remain hot for six hours. Six ounces of tea were used to make five gallons of the beverage. The trolley can serve 240 cups of tea in one sitting."* When it made its inaugural appearance on the prom it was said to be the first refreshment trolley to be run by a local authority. The Observer reported: *"The trolley was trundled along the lower promenade* (Bottle Alley) *and set up in one of the bays looking out to sea. First customers for tea were three girl bathers, who had come out of the water. Soon there was a small crowd round the trolley; the tea was still piping hot, even though it had been made two hours before. It is understood the trolley will now be in operation every day and will serve coffee in the mornings."*

~~V~~

Findings from the housing sub-committee, which was appointed in July to deal with the take-over of empty properties in view of the acute local housing shortage, were reported to the Council-in-Committee in September. It was stated that 498 houses had been surveyed and 309 were found not suitable to be requisitioned or could not be taken over by the council for some other legitimate reason. Notices had been served on 146 properties and 43 remained to be served; 48 properties had been taken under the requisition scheme and 25 families had already been housed in some of these, with the other properties requiring repair before they could be occupied. A council flying squad was going round, inspecting each house, to see what work must be carried out. The committee felt that four walls and a roof were better than nothing but they had not so far provided anything more than that. There were certain things, such as stoves, sinks and lavatories, which were absolutely necessary when taking over big properties to house three or four families, these things were an important consideration. The requisitioning scheme had also had the effect of stimulating landlords and 50 properties under consideration had been let by their owners.

~~V~~

The Rev George H Gibb, formerly minister of St Columba's Presbyterian Church, Warrior Square St Leonards, wrote from his parish in County Durham, to congratulate the Observer on its publication, "Hastings and St Leonards in the Front Line." This book was published by the Observer in April 1945 and was a collection of photographs, personal reminiscences and official reports of the enemy destruction of Hastings in World War Two. The Rev Gibb said: *"I fear that is it not generally recognised in the north of England, that the south coast towns though spared the mass attacks of heavy bombing squadrons, suffered grievously from sporadic raids. The book clearly reveals the extent of the damage done. My church, St Columba's, was among the buildings destroyed and it grieves me to see how many of the fine edifices of the town, both sacred and secular, have been irreparably damaged. So strict was the censorship during the war that one-time residents living elsewhere were ignorant of the damage that Hastings suffered. I hope that in time the damaged buildings will be repaired and Hastings and St Leonards will regain the charm which it always possessed."*

The prize-winning Hastings post-war tourism poster

Visitors from HMS Hastings ashore with bathing belles at the St Leonards Pool, August 1945

Shoppers buy flags at Plummer Roddis (Debenhams) to celebrate VJ Day, August 1945

Biddy Stonham entertains at a victory party on a wartime fire emergency tank in the Old Town, August 1945

HMS Hastings anchored off its namesake, September 1945

Hastings Mayoress, Mrs Blackman with the captain and crew members of *HMS Hastings*

German prisoners of war dig trenches for sewage pipes at the Rock Lane Housing Estate

October 1945

Projects on the development and re-planning of the borough, predicted to affect the lives and fortunes of Hastings residents for one hundred years, were outlined in mid-October by Sidney Little. The plan proposed that there should be sufficient accommodation in Hastings for private and business residents as well as those who wished to retire to the town. Included in the proposal was development of the principal shopping centre and a fully equipped bus station close to the shops and seafront, which was to be enhanced by new attractions for day and summer visitors as well as residents. Of considerable importance were improved roadways, to carry traffic between the present and future development areas, including those for recreational purposes; preservation of open spaces was also proposed. Most urgent of all was the redevelopment of bomb damaged and built-up areas for business and housing purposes and areas where the current development was unsatisfactory. A surprising proposal was for an area to be set aside for an aerodrome; a small airfield, which was used pre-war and in wartime emergency situations, already existed at Pebsham. One of the most controversial features of the proposals made by Sidney Little related to the area running from the boating lake eastwards, to the borough boundary. He proposed the removal of the covered car park and other buildings at the Fishmarket, to open up the view out to sea, the construction of a new promenade, for pedestrians only; the removal of unsightly buildings at Rock-a-Nore, and the construction of a sea lagoon for motor and other boats at the foot of the cliff, extending to Ecclesbourne Cliffs. In a flood of correspondence Observer readers expressed opposition to Sidney Little's plans for the development of Hastings, particularly those outlined for the Old Town. The Civic Society sent a resolution to Hastings Borough Council asking that they do nothing to destroy the character of the fishing quarter of the Old Town. Quotes from the letters expressed a similar theme: *"...I have been visiting Hastings for some years now and the greatest attraction to me is the charm of the Old Town and the fishing industry, not the promenade or fun fairs. The genuine visitor does not want to hear screeching or the same gramophone record played over and over again..."* Mrs Joan Tidmarsh of 219, The Ridge, Hastings, sent in some comments received from her husband, who was serving with the South East Asia Air Force: *"...The proposed electric train service to Ecclesbourne Glen should be immediately opposed. A cutting of rail tracks through that beautiful part would not enhance its beauty. Surely, walking there is part of the pleasure...Visitors to Hastings do not expect an imitation Blackpool, Skegness or Brighton. That's why they come to Hastings, to enjoy the elements... I notice the council have passed these resolutions but I am sure they have done so without prior consultation with the residents..."* Another letter put forward an idea, often repeated whenever an unpopular development was proposed for Hastings Old Town; Mr Leslie James, a frequent visitor to the town, suggested the new promenade should run in a westerly direction, towards Bulverhythe: *"...It would be the first attempt in this country to provide a logical solution to the problem of catering simultaneously for the new class of well-off holiday maker and the vast influx of day visitors. This scheme would provide considerable scope for the people of Hastings to build in a 20th Century manner, without wholesale architectural vandalism and not calling upon the fishermen to accept changes to their environment which might prejudice their livelihood..."* In his column, Vigilant said: *"...In view of the widespread public misgivings about the development schemes, I most strongly support the suggestion that members of the council should take the earliest opportunity to discover how far the local authority is committed to carrying them out, either wholly or in part. There may yet be an opportunity to rescind decisions taken hastily and without due regard to the feelings of the majority of the townspeople."*

~~V~~

It was announced in September that Winston Churchill, as Lord Warden of the Cinque Ports, was to receive the honorary freedom of the borough of Hastings. He had accepted an invitation, extended to him by the town council at the time of his appointment as Lord Warden in 1941, but a date for the ceremony was postponed, pending his formal installation as Lord Warden. The invitation from Hastings, the premier Cinque Port, was believed to be the first he received after his appointment as Lord Warden by King George. It was hoped that the traditional installation ceremony of Lord Warden, at Dover Castle, would take place in October 1945. In his capacity as Lord Warden Churchill was Honorary Colonel of the 5th Battalion the Royal Sussex Regiment; during a holiday in Italy in 1945 he travelled as *"Colonel Warden."*

~~V~~

On Tuesday 23rd October 1945 a Channel gale hit Hastings and raged for four days. On the third day the heaviest seas of the week battered the seafront; in the early afternoon, crowds risked their safety in 70 to 80 mile an hour winds, to watch the spectacle of the gigantic waves which flooded the promenade, leaving it littered with shingle and debris. The storm was the worst experienced in 20 years. The wind had been rising steadily since the previous weekend, and with each tide the sea rose higher over the promenade. At about 8.30am on Tuesday morning the sky darkened and for a few minutes winds estimated to be about 100 miles an hour swept across the town like a tornado. Tiles and slates were ripped off houses and windows were caved in, fences shattered and branches ripped from trees. The higher part of the town suffered the worst. In Milward Road many chimney stacks were rendered unsafe and houses had to be cordoned off to protect passers-by from being injured by falling debris. In Elphinstone Road the wind brought down a chimney, which toppled over onto Number 29, the house next door; both chimney stacks fell through the roof, killing 80-year-old Mrs Fanny Howard as she lay in bed. She was buried under tons of masonry. Police, fire and ambulance men rushed to the rescue but were not able to remove the debris quickly enough. A heavy lifting squad of the Civil Defence was called in to assist and they succeeded in removing Mrs Howard's body after an hour. Mrs Gosling, the owner of the house said: *"I was just about to go upstairs with Mrs Howard's breakfast when there was a terrible gust of wind that shook the house. Then there was a noise like an exploding bomb. I dropped the tray and ran upstairs to try and open the bedroom door but it was jammed, so I called the police."* There was an exceptionally high tide the same day and at about 12.00pm the sea overwhelmed the promenade at several points, including Carlisle Parade, Caroline Parade and Breed's Place. The water poured into Harold Place and the nearby streets; by 12.30pm the road round the Memorial was submerged in two feet of water and shops and offices were flooded. Girls took off their shoes and stockings to wade to drier spots. Shoppers were trapped and a boat was used to ferry them across the deepest water. A soldier acted as a one-man ferry; taking off his socks and boots he rolled up his trousers to his knees and carried girls to safety. Cars were trapped in the water and those who braved the flood on foot found themselves marooned on walls and traffic bollards. Others, on the seafront, were knocked over by giant waves and soaked to the skin. One woman had to be rescued from the underground toilets at Harold Place, which had filled with water. A van being driven along was caught by a huge wave and hurled across the road. The rising tide lapped at the steps of the Westminster Bank and poured into Middle Street.

The water ran past the police station and turned the cricket ground into a lake. Although the flood soon subsided, fire engines had to be used to pump the water out of the cellars of shops and offices and a considerable amount of stock was damaged, including sugar, other groceries and cigarettes. In the Old Town the boating lake was filled with seawater, which also overtook the departing funfair. Caravans were marooned and showmen's children looked out of the windows at the torrent swirling round them.

The weather did have its brighter side. After an inshore storm of this magnitude the fishermen could expect a big harvest, if they could get their boats out quickly enough when the storm abated. Such storms always drive large shoals of fish to the shore, especially mackerel. A story circulated that a woman who had gone out to buy fish for her husband's dinner was prevented from reaching the shop by the floods. She was just turning back when a rush of water reached her feet; when it receded she saw a sea bass struggling on the pavement, so she put it in her shopping bag to take home for dinner. The following day, despite a high tide there was no serious flooding but shopkeepers had boarded up their doors in anticipation. Many businesses around the Memorial speedily got over the problems caused by flooding. On Tuesday, the Pillar Bar in the Queen's Hotel had been two feet deep in water, with chairs and tables floating around. By Thursday evening customers were sitting in the bar and there was nothing to indicate that anything had happened. On Friday afternoon, at high tide, heavy seas once again washed over the promenade between the Queens Hotel and the Cinema de Luxe and workmen were busy trying to prevent the water inundating the streets once again. A house in Pelham Street, which had previously been damaged by enemy action, was so weakened by the gale that parts of it had to be removed for public safety. Alarm was caused at West St Leonards on the same day when it was found that a mine had washed ashore, west of the Marina Bathing Pool, on an early hour's high tide. The police sent for mine experts, who arrived just before noon, to find that the detonator section of the mine was buried in the sand. Securing the mine to prevent it washing away, they waited till the tide turned. They dug a hole in the sand alongside the mine, enabling it to be turned over and the detonators removed. A lorry hauled the mine off the beach. Occupants of properties in an area of 500 square yards of the spot were advised to evacuate their homes as a safety measure.

November 1945

Hastings' first post-war local elections were held on 1st November; Labour gained three seats on a small poll, estimated at 50%, and giving the council a composition of 21 independents and 9 Labour members. Councillor F G Philcox, returned for Hollington, said: *"At last Labour has beaten the Tory machine at Hollington for the first time in 20 years; now that we have made Hollington a Labour seat we will keep it."* The low turnout set off a spate of letters to the Observer about voter apathy and its reasons, Captain W J Cheek stating: *"At the Civic Society meeting of the All Saints Ward only 32 voters turned up. This state of apathy is very bad for all progress in this town. It makes me wonder sometimes if voters really know what their civic duty is to the council and whether they know the meaning of rates and taxes, how they are obtained and what they are used for. I sincerely hope the voters will reflect on what I have said and take a lively interest in the candidates who are to represent them for the reconstruction of Hastings."* Cecil Grocock of 3 The Pinders, Hastings, pointed out in his reply that with regard to the apparent electoral apathy, consideration should be given to the stormy weather that prevailed during the period of the meetings.

~~V~~

Prior to the installation of Hastings' new mayor, there was a frank discussion by the council on the traditional mayor making ceremony. Councillor Riddle called for the White Rock Pavilion event to be discontinued, saying that he had never been enamoured of it: *"It interferes with the administration of the staff and civic business should be done in the council chamber. It is time that some of this snobbery was dropped; the installation of the mayor is being made into nothing less than a burlesque."* Councillor F Chambers agreed and was delighted to see the motion on the agenda: *"I would like to see children of the borough interested in the work of the council and the town, if it is indeed possible for the mayor-making to interest them. But it should be done in a much more educational way than by taking them to the White Rock Pavilion, to witness what has been described to me as the Kentucky Minstrels, without the make-up. In the town hall there are some interesting objects and the children could see the start of council business before it gets into any acrimonious discussions."* Councillor Riddle suggested that the children found more amusement than interest in the ceremony, a notion refuted by Councillor H J Stephenson, a former teacher, who said that the children were not only impressed and interested but wrote pleasing essays on the subject. Councillor H C Burgess expressed bitter disappointment with the mayor-making, seeing it as haphazard and not well presented. He said: *"I would like to see the whole thing set out in the pavilion, even if it meant taking along the council tables. There is a great deal to be said for giving the people a civic sense."* Alderman T S Dymond referred to a time when the mayor-making took place in Hastings Magistrates' Court (now Hastings Information Centre): *"It was a most unsatisfactory place in my opinion, where it is impossible to have any dignity. I do not agree with the way proceedings have been conducted in the pavilion, with the council seated on the platform and the audience below."* Councillor Rymill said that the big failing at the pavilion was the amplification; the speeches from the platform could not be heard by the audience. Councillor Ford said: *"The proceedings at the White Rock Pavilion may have excited a certain amount of disdain and ridicule among some of the townspeople but the majority thinks it is a ceremony that should be preserved. There is a great deal of drabness in the world today and I am against throwing away the little piece of the borough's history and tradition that is left to them."* So it was with traditional ceremony, on 8th November 1945, that a new mayor, Councillor Frank William Chambers OBE, was elected and installed, in front of an assembly of hundreds of local citizens at the White Rock Pavilion. The Observer reported: *"The floor of the main hall was set out in the customary manner of a council meeting at the town hall, instead of being on the stage as in previous years. Flowers, foliage and ornamental plants banked in front of the stage made a charming setting for the picturesque civic scene. Spectators were grouped round three sides and watching from the balcony were children from local schools."*

On the morning of 19th May 2010, mayor-making took place at the White Rock Theatre in the presence of the Cinque Ports' Mayors, representatives from Hastings European twin towns, local dignitaries, members of the public and school children. Auditorium seating gave way to trestle tables, creating a facsimile of a council chamber. The stage and auditorium floor were decorated with floral displays in red, blue and gold, the borough colours. The Hastleons, a fund-raising amateur dramatic group, had set up the orchestra pit for that night's opening of *"Beauty and the Beast";* a Hastings Borough Council logo-screen stood in front of black curtains, concealing the theatrical backdrop for the evening show. It was in part a form of show that took place that morning, as the mayor and the council processed in out of the auditorium at various points in the ceremony, each time to the strains of *The Trumpet Voluntary*. Speeches were made by the outgoing Conservative Mayor, Maureen Charlesworth and several councillors, paying tribute to her hard work during four years in office. Councillors from both sides of the floor proposed and seconded a candidate for the next mayor; the sole Liberal Democrat, Councillor Richard Stevens, a former mayor, made an eloquent plea that the incoming majority of Labour councillors put aside the desire to elect one of their own and give the very worthy Conservative Deputy Mayor, Mrs Eve Martin, at least one year in the role of mayor. He ended with the words, *"Or do honour and decency not count for as much as they used to amongst us?"* Voting followed and a Labour Councillor, Ms Kim Forward, a former school teacher, was elected mayor, with Labour Councillor Alan Roberts as her deputy. In an interval during the ceremony children from local schools entertained with music and song. Throughout, Hastings Town Crier, Jon Bartholomew, in red, blue and gold regalia, acted as Master of Ceremonies. After witnessing the mayor-making, Victoria Seymour pondered: *"How would the 1945 council have viewed the 21st Century-style mayor-making ceremony? Was there an absence of snobbery that would have satisfied Councillor Riddle or sufficient history and tradition to please Councillor Ford? One thing that is certain, Councillor Rymill would have approved of the amplification.*

~~V~~

On Sunday 11th November 1945 the war dead of Hastings and St Leonards were honoured with the deep solemnity one might expect after the ending of a terrible war. Churches were crowded and the customary parade service was held at Holy Trinity, under the auspices of the British Legion. In the evening a Festival of Remembrance took place at the White Rock Pavilion, with hundreds attending. At the conclusion of the festival poppy petals fluttered from the ceiling of the theatre onto the assembly below, who, in silence, remembered not only those who had been lost in the military conflict but the 154 citizens who had died as a result of WWII enemy action in Hastings and St Leonards. The Observer reported: *"The last scene of homage to the men and women of the borough who had died for freedom in two world wars was ushered in by a lament, played by a Highland piper. As the bugler played the Last Post, the nine standards of the ex-service associations were lowered. The final words were a rallying call from the Rural Dean: 'Sons of this place let this be said, that we who live are worthy of our dead.'"*

~~V~~

A welcome home and re-union party was organised at the Queen's Hotel by Mrs Tyler for 50 Hastings men who had served in the 14th Army. Many of the men present had taken part in the famous crossing of the Irrawaddy River; some had been repatriated after being prisoners of war and others recently demobilised. Formal speeches were few, most of the evening being given over to entertainment. Each man was given a box of cigarettes and a ten shilling note. In a short speech Hastings Mayor said: *"When Mrs Taylor told me she was organising the party I though it was a grand idea. The Fourteenth Army had been called the Forgotten Army but they were not forgotten by the people of Hastings. Next spring, when more serving forces are back home, there will be a civic welcome to all the returned men and women, honouring them for what they have done."* Mrs Tyler was presented with a scarf, emblazoned with a badge in the South East Asia Command colours, a gift from the wives, mothers and sweethearts of the Hastings men in the Fourteenth Army.

~~V~~

The Hastings Education Committee discussed an innovative measure: that schools should keep record cards on all pupils; it was suggested that these should be purchased and put to use immediately in the local Modern, Junior and Technical Schools. Alderman Riddle pointed out that there was serious side to the matter of keeping record cards on school children, asking: *"Who is going to be able to take advantage of the history of the child that the cards would reveal? If a child was apprehended for delinquency, would the police be allowed to see the child's record card? Would the school be in a position to say no?"* The Chief Education Officer, Mr Norman King, said that the cards would be available for any confidential enquiry made by the parent; they would not be available to the police except on subpoena. Views were expressed that the reports could be used to, *"damn a boy's future"*, and that they would be one-sided and not give a complete picture and would need an additional report by an educational psychologist if they were to be a real record. Alderman Mrs Foxon assured: *"The cards would be confidential and the property of the school and they would have four or five independent judges, as each teacher would make a contribution to the card."* The proposal was passed and the system of pupil record cards installed in schools

~~V~~

A correspondent to the Observer complained about the unfairness of the food points system; these were issued in addition to the ration cards and enabled the housewife to buy off-ration foodstuffs, selecting which she wanted in accordance with the number of points she was allocated each week. A family of two parents and three children would have 25 points per week, while a single person had only five, putting many items beyond their reach, for example golden syrup, a small tin of which required 8 points. The problem of food supplies in general prompted Hastings' new MP to raise a question in the House on the subject. He asked the Minister of Food if he was aware of the shortage of groceries in Hastings, especially soap, vinegar, biscuits, cornflour and custard powder, and if he would take steps to ensure the area had fairer supplies. The minister said that from his enquires he learned that the town received its proper share and more was not forthcoming. Some of the shortages may have been due to the zoning of goods deliveries, to save on transport costs. It was announced in December 1945 that from April 29th 1946, the wartime system of zoning would cease to affect biscuit manufacturers; from that date they would be free to send their products to any part of the country. The supply, however, would continue to be governed by the availability of raw materials and the amount of labour allowed to the industry.

~~V~~

On the 27th November, at Old Church Road, Hollington, Mayor Chambers laid the foundation stone of the first pair of houses to be erected in Hastings since the war. They were built on the site of two homes that had been destroyed by a flying bomb in July 1944. The houses were being constructed by apprentices, under a local training scheme. The mayor was accompanied by Mr A C Bossom, MP for Maidstone, who was the English architect responsible for many skyscrapers in New York and other American cities. The mayor said that the 18 boys who built the Hollington houses would be very proud of their work in future years. The town council was so pleased with the standard of work that it had arranged for a further three pairs of houses to be erected under the scheme. The 27th November proved to be a busy day for the mayor. He also attended the ceremony to re-name the former Central Hotel, next door to the town hall. The hotel had been popular with US servicemen in the war; thus its new name, *"The GI",* chosen as tribute to the American forces and their friendly associations with the British people. A number of local dignitaries were present, as were representatives of the management of Whitbread and Co, along with members of the American Army, some of whom were taking back English brides to the United States. Sergeant William Hastings, of Fort Worth, Texas, aged 25 and recently married to Joyce Hopwood, an English girl, had been chosen for the duty of unveiling the pub's new sign, depicting a smiling GI. The traffic was halted in Queen's Road, as Sergeant Hastings lowered the Union Jack and the Stars and Stripes draping the sign. A post-ceremony lunch was presided over by Mr Sidney O Neville, a descendant of the Companions of the Conqueror. Among others, architect Bossom spoke at the lunch reception: *"The greatest hope of the world today is that our present understanding with America will continue and that there will be an unshakeable friendship between the United States and Great Britain. If the British and American people remain bonded together, the chance of another world war will be mainly eliminated but if they are not bonded it would be almost a certainty."* Sergeant Hastings was given a postcard-sized reproduction of the original pub sign, which he carried in his wallet for years, hoping to find someone who could tell him more about the pub; his approach to a Hastings website in 2000 brought the story to light once more. The Observer of 1945 wrote that Sergeant Hastings was presented with a silver tankard, engraved with the pub sign and an inscription but William said in 2000 that he never actually received it. *"Probably picked up by one of the old guys at the reception"*, was his pithy remark. In 2001, his children commissioned an American artist to make a copy of the pub sign and it now hangs in the ex-sergeant's home, in Fort Worth Texas; a memento of a unique event.

~~V~~

After a trip to England, Alistair Cooke, the British-born journalist and broadcaster, returned to the United States on the Queen Mary with 2,000 GI brides. Perhaps the newly-wed Joyce Hastings was among them. Cooke recounted the experience in his first broadcast of the 58-year-running BBC radio programme, *"Letter from America."* *"...I recall the majestic liner thundering its great horn as we slipped away from the dock at Southampton. All the mothers were clinging to the rail and all the babies were clinging to their mothers along the entire curving length of the ship's main deck. The ship turned about and we headed into the Channel, England faded into the night and we all went below. For the brides there was a first small shock of*

Americana; a meal with real meat and a strange vegetable; a cooked mixture of lima beans and sweetcorn, an American Indian favourite christened by them 'succotash' At the breakfast next day, there were eggs and bacon, sausage meat patties and pancakes with maple syrup. The butter was fresh and plentiful and there were oranges to take away. This went on for five days and it struck me by the second day out that few ironies of peace can be so delicate as the sight of the GI brides, comparatively famished for five years, refusing most of these goodies, not because of the rolling wave, but because over five years their stomachs had shrunk.

December 1945

In early December Hastings has its first post-war allocation of oranges, the allowance being one pound of oranges per ration book. A greengrocer's shop assistant told the Observer of their experience regarding the allocation system. (Customers did not have to register with just one greengrocer, as was compulsory in the case of butcher and grocery shops.) *"I believe that a government order exists that oranges must be sold to any person producing a ration book. But I found that many people came to our shop from other districts in Hastings, so there were not enough oranges left for our regular customers. I know that people have the right to buy their fruit where they like but it causes anger and disappointment when we have no oranges left for our regulars. I appeal to Hastings residents: In fairness to all, when the next allocation of oranges arrives, go only to your regular shop. Rationing is a nightmare to shopkeepers and customers alike and we long for its ending."* The last vestiges of food rationing, namely of meat and bacon, would not be removed until July 1954.

~~V~~

Formal steps were taken by Hastings Town Council to authorize the conferment of the Freedom of the Borough on Field Marshall Sir Bernard Montgomery, *"In recognition of his eminent and distinguished services to the British Commonwealth, Empire and allies, during the greatest war in history."* The honour was also extended to Mr D W Jackson, the retiring town clerk, for his distinguished and outstanding services to the borough for 25 years and his conduct of its considerable parliamentary and ministerial business. The double ceremony was fixed to take place on 8th March 1946. A reader wrote to the Observer saying that although he had the utmost respect for Mr Jackson, a person of Field Marshall Montgomery's significance he should not be expected to share the ceremony.

~~V~~

Before the inception of the National Health Scheme the less well-off in the community were often obliged to turn to benevolent organisations for medical care. One of these was the Hastings Free Dispensary, which was established in the town in 1842, in the former Royal Oak Pub at the bottom of the High Street. A deed was drawn up by William Lucas Shadwell, Musgrave Briscoe and other local worthies, stating that the premises be used for a free dispensary, *"For the relief and benefit of all classes of sick people, either as a separate establishment or in connection with any hospital or infirmary."* The dispensary did not close its doors during the war, despite being seriously damaged by enemy action on 23rd May 1943. Immediate repairs were carried out but the building was not scheduled for more extensive work until the war was over. A total of 621 people attended the dispensary in 1944; these required 3,886 bottles of medicine and 1,642 dressings; two operations were also carried out. During the war there was a falling off of donations to the dispensary, so the Observer published an appeal for funds in its 15th December issue: *"Few people understand what such a place means to the poor people of the town. Although Lucas Shadwell and members of the Dispensary Trust have long since passed away, there are still men anxious to extend the care the Old Town Hospital gives to its many patrons. In 1926, structural alterations and decorations were carried out and additional medical and surgical appliances were installed. Since then, no improvements have been made to meet the present day needs or to support the increase in numbers of patients from all parts of Hastings. Subscriptions can be sent to the Westminster Bank or to the collector at the dispensary."* As it transpired, the installation of the National Health Scheme, just over two and a half years distant, ended the life of the dispensary; it was used as the Old Town Clinic and NHS offices. It is now closed and unoccupied.

~~V~~

Major J Manwaring Baines, the curator of Hastings Museum since 1935 and one of the most influential figures in the matter of recording and stimulating interest in Hastings history returned to his post in December. The Observer of that year informed, with a tone of untypical levity, *"The major is related to Old King Cole, being descended, on his mother's side, from King Coel of Godebod, Ruler of Britain."* There was much work to be done on the museum building, as it had been damaged in the bombings of the nearby Royal East Sussex Hospital, Holmesdale Gardens and other sites in the locality. Mr Baines said that he was very glad be back at the museum. He had joined the army in 1940, after a spell in the Police Reserve and was then posted to a Dover field artillery unit and into the thick of *"Hellfire Corner"*, awaiting Hitler's invasion, sustaining, as he said, *"Nothing worse than a few shrapnel grazes."* Mr Baines, by then a major, was sent to Scotland, where the quiet was a remarkable contrast to Dover, but a motorcycle accident gave him a long spell in hospital. It was during this enforced break from duty that the idea germinated in his mind for his book on the history of Hastings. During his army service Mr Baines turned his scientific knowledge and ingenuity to good account, devising improved military equipment. He invented a new form of gas mask, which was brought to the attention of the government, but for production reasons it was not found practical to adopt the Baines Model. He also invented a device to enable field gunners to gauge if they could satisfactorily clear the crests of hills; another wartime invention of his was a simple buckle for equipment. Baines' book *Historic Hastings* was first published in 1955 after 13 years of research and has been reprinted a number of times; it remains the definitive history of the town. In his preface to the book Baines refuted the idea that it is a true history of Hastings, as so many historical documents were lost, quoting as an example the ancient rate books, which were sent for salvage during the war. Worse still, at the start of the war, the town's records, against advice, were stored in Hastings Caves, where they underwent deterioration from the effects of damp. Baines saying that the degree of damage to the records was, *"As if hundreds of years had passed."* Yorkshire man Manwaring Baines retired from his post as Curator of Hastings Museum in 1973 but was called back to help out on several occasions and was active in local historical societies. He died June 2002, aged 91. He had been living with his wife Sarah in the historic Hastings House. His coffin was draped with the family coat of arms, presented on the field of battle by Henry VIII in 1543.

~~V~~

The unavailability of luxuries promised that Christmas 1945 would be a rather low-key affair, as far as feasting and gifts were concerned. Judging from the Observer, post-war retailers did not seem inclined to spend much on advertising goods that they knew would be snapped up by desperate shoppers. Mastins, one of Hastings leading department stores, published a gift suggestion list; those requiring precious clothing coupons were; knitted and Astrakhan gloves; a few pairs in real fur, stockings and wool scarves. Coupon-free items were lampshades, cushions, aprons, shopping bags and felt shoulder bags. A few lucky people were able to buy the first real

Christmas trees for five years. "Vigilant" viewed the coming festivities as a salvage opportunity, informing his readers: *"If each family in the country puts out an extra half pound of clean, waste paper it would make 40 million sugar cartons or 12 million sheets of plasterboard, enough to put ceilings on 12,000 homes."* The prospects of there being much extra paper in households were doubtful; festive wrapping paper, decorations and crackers were in very short supply.

The choice of Christmas entertainment met all tastes: At the White Rock Pavilion, on the 21st and 22nd December, the National Association of Local Government Officers put on the pantomime *"Goody Two Shoes"*, a visiting company was to follow after Christmas, presenting *"Mother Goose"* in the traditional panto season. Between these two offerings the Court Players staged a performance of *"A Party for Christmas"*; seats starting at two shillings and sixpence. The De Luxe Cinema was showing the appropriately titled *"Together Again"*, the Gaiety had a double programme of *"Snow White and the Seven Dwarfs"* and *"Fantasia"*, the Kinema screened *"The Sign of the Cross"* and at the Roxy, *"The Adventures of Tom Sawyer"* was on the bill. Ore Place held a Social Club Dance and Whist Drive and St Clements Church put on a concert of Christmas Music from Handel's *"Messiah."* The management of the White Rock Baths conceived an unusual idea for a Christmas treat; throwing open the premises to the public so that they could inspect parts of the premises not usually on view, such as the engine room. A Christmas morning dip at the baths was included in the fun. Many people planned to go to Battle to see the meet of the East Sussex Foxhounds on Market Green. Hotels and restaurants did not advertise Christmas menus; rationing precluded seasonal over-indulgence.

~~V~~

Participants in pre-Christmas jollities were two pairs of honeymooners, beneficiaries of free, local hospitality after winning a national newspaper competition. Captain Cheek and his wife offered rooms in their home, a large and comfortable flat in Palace Chambers on Hastings seafront, as accommodation to the two pairs of newlyweds, in what the captain described as: *"A gesture, to make up as far as possible, to two men who had been Japanese prisoners of war."* The lucky winners spent the weekend in gracious rooms, overlooking broad views of the English Channel, enjoying breakfast in bed and all the seasonal hospitality the town could offer. The couples were Sergeant Ernest Laws, Royal Signals, and his wife Jean, of

Newcastle, and Private Turton and Anne, of West Bromwich; neither couple had been to the south coast before. Sgt Laws only learned of competition when he and his fiancée were out walking and a small boy, a complete stranger to them, showed them a piece torn from a newspaper. Mrs Laws, a domestic worker, said she had not seen her fiancé, a regular soldier, for ten years, until he was repatriated 12 months previously; the couple had become engaged by letter in 1940 when he was stationed in Singapore, which fell to the Japanese in February 1942. He was then sent to Japan as a POW, where 60 out of the 290 in the prison camp died. Sgt Laws said that one of his comrades made a radio which was kept hidden from the Japanese in a bully beef box. He said: *"We could hear London clearly; the Japs never knew we had the radio."* Private Turton, a printer in civilian life, was also captured in Singapore and survived six months of working on the notorious *"Railway of Death"*, constructed through jungle territory, from Siam to Burma, on which many prisoners of war and forced labour workers died. He said: *"The Japanese soldiers treated us terribly, but things were a little better when civilians were in control."* Also with Captain and Mrs Cheek for a brief stay over the holiday was their son, an RAF officer who won the DFC during the war. Captain Cheek served in the 1914-1918 war and in 1939 he went to France with the 1st Division, as personal cipher officer to General Alexander.

~~V~~

The Marina Sun Lounge, situated on the St Leonards seafront, was described at the time of its construction as, the finest winter facility in England. It was declared opened on Saturday 17th December 1938, without any particular ceremony, the latest stage in the town's 1930s seafront improvement scheme. A number of London and provincial press representatives visited the improvements and joined Hastings Mayor, Borough Engineer Sidney Little, who was the scheme's innovator, councillors and other local notables, for an informal lunch at the ill-fated Albany Hotel. The mayor gave what must have been one of the floweriest speeches of his career, with references to buds and blossoms, while Little stuck to practicalities, pointing out that the new structures had facilities for winter visitors: *"Today we have a bitterly cold wind and no sun and yet you will find that people can sit in the seafront shelters all day."* Little's latest scheme had added a 1,000 foot extension to the underground car park, a new lower promenade, suntrap shelters, six chalets and the glass-fronted sun lounge. It was 200 feet long and 20 feet wide, with a circular bastion or bay. The lounge could accommodate 500 at tables or 1,000 in audience seating. The floor was patterned jarrah wood and oak and the ceiling reinforced concrete, a building material for which Little had an inordinate fondness. The back of the central portion of the building was constructed from glass bricks, which could be illuminated by coloured lights. The underground car park was accessible directly from the lounge. As history tells us, the Marina Sun Lounge enjoyed less than a year of business following its opening. It had an eventful career during the war: It was taken over by Commodore Critchley, as a training base for RAF Cadets and later, when bombing made the town unsuitable as a training ground and invasion was expected, the sun lounge was converted into a strong-point. Made formidable with steel plates and concrete it was frequently machine-gunned by enemy aircraft. Although by Christmas 1945 the interior of the lounge had regained some of its pre-war attractiveness, the bullet marks and exterior war damage to the building remained, due to lack of materials and labour. The Marina Sun Lounge saw its first post-war audience on 22nd December 1945, with a concert by the well known radio saxophonist, Claude Cavolotti and his orchestra, who had been playing there on the morning of Sunday 3rd September 1939, when war was declared and the first air raid siren sounded. Cavolotti, who during the war ran the dance band of the No 11 Group Fighter Command, RAF, opened the concert by saying that it was a pleasure to return to the Marina Sun Lounge and reminded the audience he was playing selections from *"Romaine"*, to cheer up the audience, who had just been told that war had been declared, when in dashed a female air raid warden to tell then to stop the concert and disperse, as the siren had sounded. Cavolotti said, *"I feel it is fitting to open our programme today with those same selections from 'Romaine', which were so rudely interrupted."*

Sergeant William Hastings, United States Army, with his English bride, Joyce Hopwood

Hastings Town Centre floods, October 1945

Mayor-making at the White Rock Pavilion, November 1945

The Sun Lounge with Marine Court in the background, date unknown

Mr Hearnshaw at work in the Free Dispensary, High Street, Hastings Old Town

Hastings brothers Sgt: C W Ayton and Sgt: L A Ayton, British Army of the Rhine, and children, on Operation Christmas Tree, December 1945

The Children

"At last, we could all sleep in peace in our own beds"

Maureen Charlesworth

Maureen Charlesworth, former Mayor of Hastings, was born in Ilford in February 1939, two miles from the Thames and behind the Plessey factory. She said of her wartime years:

"The siren from the factory gave us a three minute warning of when the enemy planes were coming, as they were following the river to London. I still shiver when I hear a siren go off, even if it is only practice. I remember going shopping with my mother one day when it sounded; we were quite a long way from home and I started screaming with fear. It was the only time I remember being smacked. My mother did it to bring me out of the hysterics so we could hurry home to safety. We had a large Anderson shelter in the garden and my sister and I slept in its bunk beds. The shelter was equipped with food and water and a paraffin stove; I remember the smell to this day! On most nights my sister, Pat, and I would go to our own beds and when the

siren sounded Mum and Dad carried us down to the shelter for the rest of the night. My father was severely diabetic, having to have two injections each day. Even so, he passed two medicals for the RAF. The third medical revealed his condition and he was not allowed to join up. He became the night watchman for our street, as well as doing a full-time job in the East End. He was head of personnel for the whole of the London Co-op; each day he had to find out which shops were still standing and sort out the staffing, how many employees were still alive and available to man the stores. When ill health forced him to leave the job it took three men to handle the work he had done.

My sister and I used to stand in our garden and watch the dog-fights in the skies around us, until Mum came in to call us to safety. Right up until we left that house in 1959 Dad used to dig up bits of shrapnel from the garden. We were eventually bombed out in 1944 by a V2 rocket, which blew in the back of the house, on top of Mum, my sister and me. We both have scars to this day from cuts caused by flying glass. We were evacuated to Luton but we didn't stay long, as the back of our house had been shored up, so that we could live in the down and upstairs front rooms. It was a bit cramped, living and eating in one room and very cold, so the smelly paraffin heater was called into service. While we were in Luton, Dad had stayed at home, living in the Anderson shelter, and this was when he contracted TB. He was sent to a sanatorium in Brentwood, where he spent periods of time over the following seven years.

My little sister and I always walked to school, joining with other children on the way. When we were going home, if we saw horse manure in the road, we would rush to get a bucket and shovel and go back and collect it for the garden and to put on my Dad's chrysanthemums, which were his passion. He eventually got a greenhouse to grow tomatoes and cucumbers, with other vegetables in the garden, where we all helped. Failing health obliged him to give up his allotment. It was the everyday job of my sister and me to dust the house, clear the grate and lay the fire every morning, to light when we got in from school. We also kept chickens in the garden and my sister and I went every morning to find the eggs. My Mum could never kill the chickens and had to get a neighbour to wring their necks."

Because Maureen's father was in hospital so frequently it involved many long journeys by bus for her mother on visiting days. Her daughters were left in the care of their stern Great Aunt Hettie, a woman who knew nothing about children and had a tendency to shout at them. She taught Maureen to cook and by the age of 12 she could produce a Sunday lunch. She only rarely saw her Dad during his time in the chest hospital and she recalls visiting him each Boxing Day, to find him in a ward exposed to the elements, with snow on the floor and bed. This fresh air treatment was standard for TB patients at that time.

"Of course, he lost his job and times became very hard but we children didn't really notice. We had fruit, vegetables and chickens in the garden and Mum would swap any surplus with the neighbours. She always had jars of bottled fruit and salted runner beans, Pat and I looked after the carrots, stored in a tin bath in the shed and kept an eye on the strings of onions. We didn't waste a thing, a concept I used when I ran a hotel, always keeping a stock pot. I remember the VE and VJ Street parties. Everybody's parents managed to make fancy dress outfits; my sister was a fairy and I was a nurse, the pinafore had a large red cross on the bib; we felt so proud. How the families were able to provide food for these parties I do not know but they were occasions to remember."

On leaving school, proficient in French and Spanish but unable, for financial reasons, to take up further education to become a teacher as she had hoped, Maureen got a job at Lloyds Bank in West Smithfield, near the meat market and St Bartholomew's Hospital. When the family moved Lloyds transferred Maureen to their St Leonards Silverhill Branch where she advanced her career, working at several East Sussex branches, ending up as Chief Cashier in Silverhill. Maureen then moved into the hotel business with the parents of her husband Terry, eventually running the Yelton Hotel on Hastings Seafront, with Terry as manager and Maureen company secretary. She said that her years in the bank helped with managing the books, doing the wages and dealing with bookings and guests. Maureen and Terry went on to run the cafeteria and bar at the Summerfields Sports Centre; then they bought the Mayfair Hotel, which they ran for 17 years, until retirement in 1999. After her husband died, Maureen returned to her involvement with local politics, becoming a councillor again and then deputy mayor to Pam Brown. Now grandmother to her son Mark's and daughter-in-law Amanda's twins, Luke and Amy, she said of her last six years: *"They have been the best of my life. Being mayor is a wonderful job and I have enjoyed every minute of it, meeting amazing people, many of whom are doing so much to help others less fortunate than themselves, and being part of so many events that will always be in my memory."*

Ruby Henderson

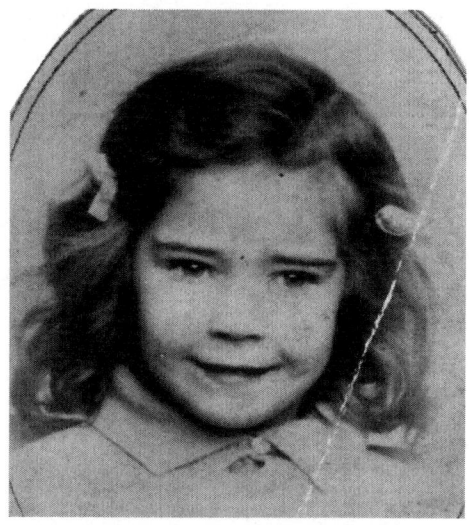

Ruby, rising seven in 1939

Hastings resident Ruby Henderson was born in Brockley, near Lewisham and in 1939, at the age of six, she was evacuated to Camber Sands, Near Rye, aged six, along with her 11-year-old brother. The photograph of Ruby was taken at Lucas Street School Deptford London: *"I have a vague recollection of initially sleeping in a beach hut and then being boarded with an elderly couple who were horrible. My brother and I ran away from there and although we were soon traced we had made our point about being unhappy and were moved to Hastings, living in different but neighbouring houses in Bohemia Road. I think I have recently identified the houses but it seems there are no official records of this kind of thing to back it up."*

When Hastings came under the threat of being a landing point for the expected German invasion, Ruby and her brother returned to their family, and were evacuated yet again, to Weston-super-Mare: *"These days I look at six year-old children and wonder how people would cope today with sending such little ones away to strangers, how did our parents do it, how could they let us go? It's left me as the kind of person who does not like to go away, even for a few days. Going on holiday doesn't interest me, it seems like a chore. In the war my mother collected tips for extending the meagre rations; she cooked whale and horse meat and I was quite happy to eat it as a Sunday roast. I got into trouble with my early cooking attempts, substituting bicarbonate of soda with Andrew's Liver Salts.*

Ruby was very aware that the war was coming to an end, saying that having two older brothers in the services heightened her anticipation: *"We did have a street party but I do not remember it clearly. There was probably not much food but in those days people tended to share what they had. I left school at 14 and had various jobs in a shop, office and factory, ending up in Barclay's Bank, where I stayed for ten years. I realised it was the kind of job I was really suited for and should have taken in the first place. I married aged 19 and have two children. My husband died a few weeks after our Golden Wedding day."* What was Ruby's abiding memory of victory? *"At last, we could all sleep in peace, in our own beds."*

Dorothy Morris

Dorothy's Tackleway victory party. August 1945

Not every victory child had strong memories of WWII: Many accepted war as part of normal life, with events in the home leaving more lasting impressions than the conflict. In the wartime recollections of Dorothy Morris, (nee Reeves), born in 1934 at 21, Brewery Cottages, (now Roebuck Street) Hastings Old Town, it is her early family life she recalls the most vividly. Dorothy was the sixth child in of a family of eight and due to overcrowding at home she slept at her grandmother's house in Wood's Passage:

"Stories of the properties in that area being like slums are true. Our cottage had holes in the walls and floors but other houses were in a much worse condition than ours, so we thought we were well off. My father worked in Watney's Brewery Yard in the Old Town; he was not eligible for war service as he had suffered a serious injury when he fell among broken glass at the brewery and the tendons of his arm were cut. He was also employed as a boy ashore, winching in the fishing boats, working at times for Bert White, the father of Deeday White. My father died of a heart attack, on the beach,

aged only 48. My mother was employed at Catt's Laundry, Silverhill and also took in washing at home, as did her mother. To earn a little extra money for the family I would be sent round neighbours' houses to sell fish at a shilling a plate." Dorothy has only two enduring memories of war in Hastings: One is of 23rd May 1943, when bombs fell in the High Street, just a matter of yards from their home: *"My little brother was sitting in his high chair and when the bombs exploded my mother fell to the floor in a faint. The other time was when my little sister and I were going to the pie shop in George Street and we had to take cover in Strong's Passage, as a German plane was machine-gunning the town. My older brother was in the Devonshire Light Infantry and took part in the D-Day landings and also fought in Italy. He suffered a number of wounds during the invasion and carried pieces of shrapnel in his body until he died aged 84."* Dorothy says of her growing up years that there was a great spirit of neighbourliness among the mothers: *"They would help each other out with food for the children when times were particularly hard. Clothes were mostly hand-me-downs, but we had an aunt living in the Croft, who made dresses from old curtains for us girls; some of the dresses were made of velvet and very pretty."*

Dorothy attended All Saints Infants and Junior School; out-of-school playtime was spent in the streets surrounding her home and in the Wilderness, gardens that surrounded the derelict Wilderness House that lay among trees, in a walled area at the top of Hastings High Street. As the photograph bears witness, Dorothy went to a victory party, put on by the Sun Inn for the children of Tackleway. She has no recollection of the event but it must have been, as the date on the photograph suggests, held to celebrate victory over Japan. At that time few families owned cameras and film was very scarce so this group picture is the only one that Dorothy has of her childhood. (She can be seen third row, third from right.) When Dorothy left school she worked at Featherstonehaugh's, the grocer in Queens Road; which became a fish and chip shop. She married Clive Morris when she was 21; the couple have three daughters, six grandchildren and ten great grandchildren. *"My family took the war very seriously but we just got on with things. I think that being brought up in a war has made me appreciate life much more."*

Clive Morris

Clive with Hastings Mayor, Maureen Charlesworth

Clive Morris was born in 1935 at Egremont Place in Halton, later moving to 136, Mount Pleasant. He has no particular memories of the beginning of WWII but said that his family evacuated from Hastings to Wiltshire in 1940:

"We stayed there only six weeks. The cottage in which we were billeted was a condemned building; when it rained the water ran in at the back door and out at the front. My mother had given birth to my first sister during the time we occupied the cottage. Returning to our house in Hastings we found the furniture covered in green mould. I remember that my second baby sister was due to be baptised at Emmanuel Church on the West Hill but on 3rdMay 1942 the vicarage was bombed and the church damaged in an evening lightning raid. The vicar's little daughter was killed in the raid. My sister was eventually baptised in Mendham Hall. My father died in the war, aged 37, of flu and pneumonia; life-saving antibiotics were not available at that time. My mother, who by then had four children, opened a secondhand shop in our house, selling almost anything on a commission basis."

Clive has a few random memories of the war: *"I saw soldiers marching in single file down either side of Mount Pleasant, with Bren gun carriers driving in the middle of the road; a VI rocket with a Spitfire in pursuit and an explosion above the Broomgrove Valley."* The date and time of this incident was Wednesday, 19th July 1944, 1.17pm: A Spitfire was chasing a V1 through the valley in an attempt to destroy it. A child eye-witness, the late Peter Paine, said: *"The rocket was suddenly enveloped in a massive cloud of black gas and golden flames and there was a simultaneous explosion. The debris fell on where the Broomgrove Estate now stands; seven people were injured."*

A more clearly remembered and personal war for Clive was the stone fights with the boys from Broomgrove. He did not go to a victory street party but recollects one that took place in nearby St George's Road. Clive did see the celebrations on the West Hill and caught a glimpse of the mayor, Alderman Blackman. Clive thought at the time that the mayor looked like Winston Churchill. After the war Clive was apprenticed to a carpenter and later did his national service in the Royal Sussex Regiment, which he joined at the age of 20; his service was deferred for two years so that he could finish his apprenticeship. Clive became a self-employed carpenter and in later years lectured at Hastings College. Clive said that he first noticed his wife-to-be, Dorothy Reeves, at the Junior Tackleway Club, where, aged 16, he was cross-country runner: *"One day I saw Dorothy get on the bus at Hastings Town Centre and followed the bus on my bicycle. When she got off at her stop at the Wilderness I asked her out. We were married four years later, just before I left for national service; I had to get my parents' permission as I was under 21."*

Clive has devoted many years to charity and voluntary work with Old Town organisations; he has served for 34 years as churchwarden at All Saints Church. He has been a trustee of the Magdalen and Lasher Charity for 39 years and for the past 21 years has taken lead responsibility for the charity's extensive portfolio of properties in Hastings and St Leonards. In 2009 Clive was granted the Order of 1066, an award that is given annually on the Battle of Hastings anniversary, 14th October, in recognition of services to the community. At the presentation in the Hastings Town Hall's Council Chamber, Mayor, Maureen Charlesworth said of Clive Morris: *"...He is caring of people in need and is not put off by problems along the way. He is a man of compassion and action, unfailingly kind, patient, cheerful and efficient."*

Gillian Kemp

Gillian Kemp with her father

Gillian Kemp, (nee Whatman) and her husband, David, a former Grenadier Guardsman, live in a Grade II listed cottage in Hastings Old Town. The house, which escaped demolition during the Old Town clearances thanks to her mother's determined stance, was Gillian's childhood home: *"My father, George Whatman, was called up as soon as war was declared, as until he married he had served in the Royal Artillery. Before the war he was a postman but prior to this he had worked on the building of Marine Court, pumping out the water and shingle on the site. After he joined up he was sent to Scotland and then, along with General Montgomery and the 8th Army, was shipped to Egypt. He went through the desert and then on to Sicily and afterwards to Italy. His unit fought at the Battle of Monte Casino and lost all its officers when trying to capture the monastery. He was in Italy when the war ended. We were so excited to think that he would be home soon, as he had been away for five years. We later saw some of our uncles and friends return but still no Dad. Then one day Mum had a letter from him saying his unit had been posted to Greece for a mopping up operation. As it transpired he was sent to Palestine. We were so unhappy that he was not coming home. I was seven years old when he left home and at the age of 12 I had won a scholarship to the high school and wanted to tell him all about it.*

I was evacuated during the war and it was not a happy experience. I was not properly fed and ended up in hospital, suffering from malnutrition. Subsequently, I was sent to a really good family and was very happy. Throughout this time my older brother, John, was with me, acting as guardian as best he could. He's 80 now. One November afternoon in 1945 I came home from school and there, sitting in the kitchen armchair, was my dad. I just threw myself into his lap for a cuddle. My Mum had tears in her eyes. Dad could not believe how much I had grown up. It was the happiest day of our lives when Dad was safely returned to us. He told us that when he took the train to come home he had not got a ticket, so instead of going through the barrier he made his way through familiar ground; the sorting office beside the railway station. He was in uniform and the postmen gave him a cheer. He went back to being a postman; some older local people may remember him. Dad had brought me a special gift from Palestine; it was a book of pressed flowers and views of Jerusalem. The book was bound in olive wood; I still have it today. At Christmas time I found he had brought me another present; it was a gold cross and chain. I gave it to my eldest daughter to wear on her wedding day and told her she could keep it.

Like many people who lived through WWII, I believe the experience affected in me in a number of ways, big and small: My mother used to fill the kettle before we went to bed in the war, in case the water mains were bombed and we needed a cup of tea. I still do that to this day! She was very capable and mended our shoes in the war and worked an allotment at the Pinders, where there are houses now. She gave me a little plot on the allotment to grow things and my love of gardening comes from that. I get no pleasure from buying clothes; I'm sure this is left over from the war when they were hard to come by. I think the experience of war made me practical and sympathetic to people's needs and led me to my career as a school social worker."

John Whatman

John Whatman with his sister Gillian

John Whatman was born in May 1930, into a Hastings Old Town very different from the place we know today. The new Bourne Road had not cut the heart out of this historic quarter and the alleys, known locally as twittens, still snaked between the houses. *"I started school at All Saints Junior School but when the war broke out I was evacuated to Welwyn Garden City with my sister Gillian, returning to Hastings in 1943 I went to Clive Vale Secondary School. My education suffered throughout the war due to crowded classrooms and periods when schooling was reduced to half of the day or none at all. In 1940 I was on the East Hill, near the twin Lewis guns, as the Battle of Britain was raging overhead. Suddenly, something hit the ground a few steps ahead of me and was buried in the soil; I do not know if it was a stray bullet or shrapnel. My friend Jimmy Whiting and I joined the Boys Brigade as buglers; our mothers soon got fed up with our "music" practice at home so we took to bugling on the East Hill. My free time was not all spent on messing about; I worked as a volunteer, assembling cast iron Morrison shelters in local residents' houses. I had a lucky escape on the Sunday morning of 23rd May 1943. I stayed at home, as I was excited at my mother's preparations for my birthday next day. She was making raspberry jelly, a treat so rare in wartime that its making warranted an audience. At the time when I would normally have been walking about Hastings Old Town with my pals, a lightning air raid took place, which demolished the Swan Inn and a number of other Old Town properties, with considerable loss of life. When I did go out I could hear survivors under the wreckage, crying out for help. I also saw, piled on the seafront gardens, the remains of the Albany Hotel, in which many Canadian Soldiers were killed in the same raid.* (A permanent reminder of the Swan Inn tragedy can be seen in Hastings Old Town High Street. A commemorative garden now stands on the former site of the Swan Inn, demolished in the Sunday lunchtime air raid.)

John did not find his wartime childhood an adventure, saying that when it started he had no conception that war could be so evil. To compensate for his inadequate education John stayed on at school until the age of 15, the leaving age then being 14. He wanted to be a post office telegram boy, enthralled with the idea of riding a motor bike, but instead he was apprenticed to a carpenter and joiner. He went to school for one night a week and on two afternoons, at the Waterloo Technical School, which was opposite to his house. From 1950 John did his two years national service at RAF at Calshot, the coastal village in Hampshire, where the RAF flying boats were docked. He used to see the big liners come in and witnessed the arrival of the *SS United States*, when it broke the world speed record for an Atlantic crossing in July 1952. On leaving the RAF John returned to his work as a carpenter and joiner with Corbins. To increase the range of his experience, John was sent to work on the houses in Churchill Avenue, as one of six carpentry apprentices selected by builders Eldridge and Cruttenden. John saved up to buy the still-coveted motorcycle, an Ariel Red Hunter. It was offering a ride home on this to Joan, a girl he met at Hastings Pier on Coronation night, which led to their marriage on 1st April 1956, a double ceremony with his sister Gillian (now Kemp) and her fiancé David.

Ron Fellows

Ron during his National Service with the Royal Fusiliers

Ron Fellows was born in Hastings in 1932 to parents who owned a succession of general and grocery stores around the town. In September 1939 they took ownership of a shop in Middle Street, which had belonged to Mr & Mrs Tilbury. On April 24th 1942 she was visiting the shop and stayed to chat, when the siren sounded. Mrs Fellows persuaded her to take shelter in the shop and that probably saved her life, as when Mrs Tilbury returned to her home at 2, Wellington Road she found that it had been demolished by a bomb in a tip and run raid.

A wartime life on the Hastings Home Front was one of narrow escapes, as Ron's childhood experiences illustrate. *"The Ministry of Food office was initially above the Woolworth's store but later it moved to Verulam Buildings, which was opposite to Hastings Pier. On a return trip from this office my brother Syd and I saw a low flying enemy aircraft coming in over the pier; as soon as we saw the plane it began to machine-gun the seafront. We hid in the passage beside Palace Chambers and it was half an hour before we could pluck up the courage to emerge."*

In an unconnected event, news circulated that that a German plane had crashed and the firemen had taken it to South Lodge at Brisco's Estate, (Summerfields.)

"Nobody had heard of health and safety regulations in those days and being an inquisitive eight year-old I went to have a look. The plane had no wings, only a fuselage on wheels. There were lots of people inside, taking bits off it. I was in the cockpit when somebody let off a gas container. Everybody got out in a hurry and I jumped from the cockpit, which was about 14 to 16 feet off the ground; fortunately, somebody caught me as I jumped; surprisingly, nobody was hurt in the panic. With my brother and I, our friends often played in the woods on the Brisco Estate; the mock Roman bath, the two lions' heads and the walled garden, still in existence, were in perfect order then. We picked the pears growing against the walls; we did not regard it as stealing as the school in the grounds had been evacuated and the place taken over by the council as offices and the Auxiliary Fire Service; later the National Fire Service was located there. The Fire Station was in Middle Street, and opposite was the garage for another vehicle."

Ron and his brother were not evacuated from Hastings in 1940; the Fellows children arrived home from school one day, bringing details about the travel arrangements and identity labels, but they refused to go, preferring to take their chance in Hastings. The family did not have an air raid shelter nor did they go to the public shelters, but went bed early to get some sleep before the drone of the German planes came over and the raids started. On one occasion Ron and his family counted as a German plane dropped 21 bombs over Hastings.

American soldiers parked their lorries in Station Road, next to Middle Street, when they visited Hastings to go to the cinema or to meet girls. The local children played in the American lorries and would ask the soldiers for sweets or chewing gum, but the American Military Police, (called Snowdrops because they wore white helmets), put a stop to this. Ron said that talking to the British and Canadian soldiers, who mounted mock battles around town and manned the gun emplacements, was a popular pastime with small boys. But they were often told to move on, reminded by the men that they were there to train and prepare to fight a war.

Two bombs fell on Havelock Road, which overlooked the front of the Fellows' shop: On the afternoon of Tuesday 8th October 1940, the Women's Voluntary Service HQ was hit, trapping one of the workers, former Mayoress Miss Phyllis Burden, in the top storey. Three fatalities resulted from this raid, one being a girl who was not found till some days later, in the ruins of a Havelock Road office. Further destruction to Havelock Road buildings occurred on May 17th 1942.

"After the huge bang caused by the bomb, our cat Nappy, (called that because he was born in Waterloo Passage, Old Town,) took off. This was Sunday dinner time, we thought we lost him for good, but we finally saw him coming home at 8.35pm, all covered in a dirty grey dust. Following one of the two occasions, I do not remember which, that Havelock Road got bombed, a couple of my friends and I went into the wrecked buildings, where to our surprise, we found a man's hand, which we took to the police station, opposite the Clarence Hotel, at the bottom of Middle Street. We gave the hand to a policeman, who said it was a chicken's foot. We asked, "Do chickens wear rings on their feet?" As the years have passed I have told people about this episode in my life and wondered if they believed me. Then, in the Hastings and St Leonards Observer, on the 4th January 2008, the same police officer, the late Ex-Inspector Charlie Banks aged 94, told his story of the very same episode. I wrote to the Observer and told them that I was one of the boys and they printed my letter. I collected shrapnel: One piece I found buried in Linton Gardens, in the tennis courts. One inch of it was sticking out of the ground and when I got hold of it, it was still very hot. so I had to go back for it. When I dug it out I found it was half an inch thick and 2 inches wide and 3 inches long, then it was turned at right angle and went on for another 10 inches, this was my best piece."

The Havelock Road bomb site, backing on to Middle Street, became an exciting but dangerous playground for Ron and his pals; they would climb the wall and run over the semi-collapsed corrugated metal roof of an outbuilding that remained after the bombing. A Conference pear tree and a mulberry tree were also left intact; Ron said the mulberries were very nice and he recalled learning about the silk worm, which eats the mulberry leaves. A 2,400 gallons emergency water tank occupied the lower part of the Havelock Road bomb site, after it was cleared of debris. The Middle Street VE party took place on this bomb site. As far as Ron can remember the food was provided by the families, the Memorial Café in Middle Street owned by

Mr and Mrs Boakes, with fruit from Paine & Rogers the wholesale greengrocer, who had a warehouse nearby.

Ron did his national service in the Royal Fusiliers, from 1951 to 1953; travelling to Germany, Malta, Libya. He was also stationed in the Tower of London, the RF depot. After being demobbed he undertook a wide variety of jobs of a practical nature, of which he said, *"I didn't have any O-Levels but given a spirit level, my two hands and common sense I could tackle most construction jobs."* He spent the last seventeen years of his working life in the civil service.

Ron is the grandson of the notable Hastings Mayor, Alderman William James Fellows, who held office for two separate periods of two years in the 1920s. As mayor, councillor and private citizen, William Fellows devoted years to his community, and also on a wide range of local committees, too numerous to mention. Following in his grandfather's footsteps Ron has worked on many committees, retiring from most of these in 2005, when he became ill. In spite of this, in 2010, he is president of the Hastings Trolley Bus Restoration Group, president of Hooe's Old Motor Club, vice-president of the Hastings branch of the Royal Sussex Regimental Association and treasurer of the Hastings Local History Group. Ron is also a volunteer steward at the Lifeboat Station for two days a week. He is keenly interested in local history and writes for various local history and community publications. A life member of Burton's St. Leonards Society, Ron often expresses regret at the loss, to so-called progress, of so many of Hastings and St Leonards' historically important buildings. Disadvantaged by having his sight damaged from contracting measles when he was three years old, Ron said that he believed the biggest effect the war had on him was the way it interfered with his early education.

Clive Upton

Clive with small friend, ready for action

Upton's Motor Upholstery is a local firm with a history spanning four generations, starting up when coaches were the main form of transport. Clive was born into the family in July 1934 at 5, Waterloo Passage; moving in 1939 to Bembrook Road, prior to the proposed clearance scheme of the Old Town. At that time the family trade was run from a Georgian stables situated at the top of Hastings High Street; the building has since been converted into the Stables Theatre. After the war began there was very little motor upholstery work around; the majority of private cars were off the road for the duration. Clive's father made gas mask cases for a while but this did not provide any kind of living. On 26th July 1940 Clive was in the Royal East

Sussex Hospital, having his tonsils removed when, at 7.15am, a lone German raider dropped a string of bombs on several locations in Hastings, including Bembrook Road, causing the town's first civilian fatality. Clive and his parents went to live in Glastonbury, where his father found a job in a factory making aircraft parts; after about 18 months the family moved to Kew in London. Beneath Kew Green there was a public air raid shelter and, along with hundreds of other Londoners, the Uptons would take their bedding down to the shelter every night. By day Clive and his pals got up to the usual pranks of the wartime boy.

"We played hopscotch, using as counters the red glass reflectors that we pinched from the entrances to air raid shelters, we made encampments on the banks of the River Thames at Kew and pestered the American soldiers at a nearby army camp site to give us chewing gum and sweets. I had a heavy, old-fashioned pre-war bike and would cycle to Richmond public swimming baths, which still maintained a policy of segregation, with males and females being obliged to attend separate sessions. My family made a brief return to Hastings to check that the house and workshop were OK; it must have been at the time of the V1 attacks. I recall walking along Braybrooke Road with my mother when a V1 was approaching and people started running to find shelter but we just kept on walking because we knew from our London experience that while the engine was running we were safe. I also remember lying in bed at night watching the searchlights scan the sky."

Clive's family returned to Hastings permanently in 1945. He said that it must have been around the time of victory over Japan being declared; he had passed the eleven plus examination and was destined for Hastings Grammar School. His father gave him the weekly task of burning the workshop rubbish. *"The nurses from the District Nurses' Home spotted the fire and came down to see what was going on, thinking it was some kind of victory celebration but it was only a little fire and soon went out."*

On leaving school Clive worked in the family business. He said that every summer a troupe of travelling entertainers rested their caravan at the rear of the stable workshop. In 1952 Clive had to sign up for National Service; on being asked which service he wanted to join, he said the Royal Sussex Regiment, in the mistaken idea they were based at West St Leonards but in fact it was the Territorial Army building he had seen: *"During my time in the army I learned and saw things of which I had previously known nothing but it was a not a happy period. My father fell gravely ill and, as an only child, I was given a compassionate discharge from the army before my two years were up. I went back to camp just one more time, to return my kit. I had rammed my uniform into my kit bag and I got a telling off from the sergeant for bring it back creased."* Reflecting on his wartime childhood Clive said that it was not until some years after that he understood how much people went without. The family business still operates but from new premises in Brunel Road, St Leonards and under the management of his son, David Upton.

Pat Upton

Pat in the family garden in wartime Hastings

Pat Upton was born in September 1936 in Fernbank Maternity Home, Old London Road Hastings, just across the road from the family home at Number 47. During WWII, Pat's father Stanley was a special constable. After the war was declared Pat's family remained in Hastings until the bombing started, when she, her parents and brother Peter went to live in Tewin, Hertfordshire. Pat clearly remembers the journey to Tewin in her father's Austin 7, with suitcases strapped to the car's roof and rear carrier. There was an air raid as they passed through London and they had to abandon the car and run to an underground shelter: *"Staying in Tewin for 18 months, we made a brief return to Hastings; I think it must have been in 1943, as I remember my father coming home from his special constabulary duties, his uniform covered in feathers; these had floated everywhere after the heavy bombing of the Old Town, when many homes and business, including a bedding store, were destroyed on 23rd May 1943. My father was devastated after what he had witnessed in the aftermath of this raid."*

Pat cannot remember the exact date but some time after this raid she, her parents and brother went to live on an uncle's farm at Hawkenbury, Tunbridge Wells in Kent, She recalls this period as idyllic: *"We were cushioned from the worst of rationing by living off farm produce and my uncle also had a butcher's shop so there was good supply of meat. That does not mean that we were unaware that the country was at war. There were three barrage balloons at Hawkenbury and one day a VI made contact with the wires, which had the effect of turning the missile right around so it was heading for our farm. Everybody shouted and sought cover inside the house, underneath the furniture. I was pushed into the cupboard under the stairs. Luckily, the VI passed over us and exploded several miles off. When I came out of the cupboard the family realised it had not been a very safe place at all, as stored household china and other crocks were hanging from hooks on the cupboard walls. I do not know the exact date we returned to Hastings but I was shocked at the destruction of so many buildings in the town. I also remember that there were rolls of barbed wire and individual blocks and great slabs of concrete on the beach; I learned later that these were tank traps and gun emplacements. The underground air raid shelters at the bottom of Torfield were still open and we children used to play in the entrances, daring each other to venture further inside, to brave the dangers we imagined existed in the darkness. I cannot remember a victory street party but I did go to a party at the Winkle Club so that may have been part of the celebrations."*

Pat, who on leaving school was employed at the education office, already knew the boy whom she would eventually marry, from having seen him about the town as they were growing up; she was formally introduced to Clive Upton at a wrestling match on Hastings Pier. The couple married in 1955 at All Saints Church in Hastings Old Town; they have a son and daughter. When asked what effect she thinks that the war had. Pat said: *"The war inspired a wonderful camaraderie in the nation and also made me appreciate what we have now."*

Peter Moon

Peter and work colleagues on the roof of the Hastings Observer Offices

The image of Peter Moon, in defiant stance on the roof of the Hastings and St Leonards Observer during WWII, typifies the spirit of the boys who grew up in those troubled times. Peter admits he did find it alarming at aged 12, when among the first bombs dropped on Hastings there were some 500-pounders, which fell on Torfield, close to his home. Never the less, he picked up the shrapnel after the bombing, to add to his collection, a popular pasttime for wartime boys. Peter was born at 5, Exmouth Place but by the time the war had started he had moved to 47, Old London Road, where his father, a builder and decorator by trade, constructed an air raid shelter of corrugated iron under the stairs. Peter worked as an apprentice reporter for the Observer from 1942 to 1944. He was to come even closer to enemy action during his working hours. He said: *"I was at Marine Court, getting copy for an Observer sports roundup from the RAF personnel, which included the well known boxer, Len Harvey, the British heavyweight, who was also billeted there, when a bomb was dropped and it damaged the top storeys of the building.* (Records show the time was 9.25am on 21st September 1942.) *There was a huge explosion; I felt lucky to have escaped with nothing worse than a bad headache."*

An Ack-Ack gun was installed on the roof of the Observer building; when the gun was fired at enemy planes carrying out tip and run raids over the town, the staff would hide under their desks.   Speaking of his workplace Peter said: *"Of course I remember the editor, Frederick William Goodsell, or FW as we termed him. He had very delicate hands; he played the piano and loved classical music. AE Smith was the head reporter; he was the organist at Emmanuel Church and I pumped the organ for him. The photo on the roof of Observer building was taken by the paper's photographer, Reynolds. The man with the pipe is Hazelden, who was general factotum about the office; I do not know the others in the photo. I recall that on the Observer staff were Dickie Downs, who went into the navy and Dengefield, from Bexhill. Photographer Reynolds was followed by Hawkins, whose Dad owned the Creamery Tea Rooms."*

Peter went to live in Tewin with his family, including younger sister Pat, also featured in this book. He said: *"We travelled in the family car, with my parents and an aunt and uncle, who were living with us at the time; my uncle's false leg was strapped to the roof of the car along with the luggage. My Uncle Otte was ex-Royal Navy and had lost a leg when serving as coxswain. A stuka dive-bombed the ship and the magazine was hit. The captain was killed so my uncle brought the ship home in spite of having had his leg blown off above the knee; he just dosed himself up with rum and put his cap over the stump of his leg; his bravery won him a DSM. He was fitted with an artificial leg at Roehampton Hospital and his experience of learning to walk was featured in an article in the London Illustrated."*

After a second evacuation to Kent, Peter and his family lived and worked on an uncle's farm at Hawkenbury, Tunbridge Wells, above which doodlebugs passed and dog fights occurred; he thought that this period of the war was both terrifying and exciting: *"You never knew what was going to fall out of the sky; we were hay-making and canon shell cases were falling down around us. On VE Day at Hawkenbury they made a guy to resemble Hitler, my father shot it and then it was set alight."* On his return to Hastings Peter thought that it looked like a ghost town; his father started work immediately on war damage repairs. Peter was in the army from 1946 to 1949. His demobilisation was delayed because of the war in Korea but he did not serve there. Peter thinks that the most profound effect of the war on his life was the ruining of his education. Before the family left Hastings he had attended the Central School, Priory Road. Subsequently, he went to small overcrowded village schools or not at all. He advanced his education post-war by going to night school.

Moya Frost

Moya with her mother and father

Moya was born in Balham, London, in 1941. Her father was not able to join the forces as he had poor eyesight so he became a police officer and was posted away from home for much of the war. Moya was evacuated to Birmingham and returned to London in time for the doodlebug raids. She recalls being at Hampton Court Palace one day when there was an air raid warning. Her father picked her up in his arms and ran for the shelter of the palace but her mother and aunts just squatted under a conifer tree, laughing and giggling.

"My parents were a devoted couple; I have a precious keepsake from when the war ended, a letter that my father wrote to my mother, promising they would never be parted again. I keep the letter on display in my home, in a frame with a photograph of my parents and me as a small child." As Moya grew older she played on the London bomb sites and remembers being hauled up by friends into the lofts of wrecked homes. She said of the war's end; *"My only memory of a victory street party is of a delicious looking pink*

blancmange that tasted terrible, as if it had been made of water; it probably was!"

Moya says that being a wartime child has left her with a strong attachment to home; although she enjoys travel she cannot wait to get back to her house. Moya reflected on the effect that the war had on her parents: *"It was not only rationing that influenced my parents' post-war lifestyle, they were very frugal people. However, when rationing finally ended, they uncharacteristically, 'went overboard', enjoying the rich food denied to the nation for so many years and which we now know to be not particularly healthy. I believe that this contributed to bringing about the conditions from which they died."*

Ron Burkin

Ron in the Royal Air Force December 1945

Ron Burkin, the author's older brother, recounts his memories of wartime and victory:

"During WWII I was not old enough and later, not fit enough for war service as I had contracted infantile paralysis (polio) *then underwent mastoid surgery aged 16. During my recovery I was sent to do a government rehabilitation and training course in instrument making, at a place near Croydon Airport. There were a number of war-wounded servicemen on the course; some were amputees. They did not get the kind of help that is given to such casualties today and so tried to help each other. On frosty mornings they would arrive at the workshop, holding each other up, laughing and joking. I admired them and felt proud to be associated with men like these. It certainly gave me something to think about. In the time following the end of the war people were saying that it was not going to be like the aftermath of the last one, with soldiers coming home to be treated like rubbish. Sadly,*

many were, but I think that the situation was improved on 1918 by the fact that we had a labour government and house building was started as soon as possible.

I can't say that I was excited in the days leading up to the announcement of the ending of the war. When it came it felt as if we had been forced to listen to loud music for a long time and suddenly it stopped, leaving us relieved and calm, with one ear cocked in case it started again. I remember VE Day alright. I was 18 years old and I went to London by train with a school mate. I wanted to go to London because my mother had lived there as a child and young woman and she told me how marvellous it was when the Great War ended and that people went crazy in the streets. My mate and I arrived at Charing Cross Station about dinner time and when we stepped outside everywhere was crammed with people. We walked for miles, including going into the Mall. Some road works had been going on there and the equipment was roped off; three Canadian soldiers were stoking up the steam roller and trying to get it going. We talked to them for a while and then cleared off. We thought that if the Canadians got the steam roller moving there would be trouble and we did not want to be part of it. People were trying to get drinks but the pubs had run out of beer. I had an idea; I went to a railway station buffet and they still had a supply but it was more expensive.

During the latter part of the war my mate and I used to go to Speakers' Corner in Hyde Park. One of our favourite speakers was the black, horse-racing tipster, Prince Monolulu, who was always dressed in African robes. It was his speciality to draw the American soldiers to the front of his crowd to bait them. By chance, we met up with the prince on VE Night and with him and my mate I started a conga line in Hyde Park, which continued into Park Lane and as far as Oxford Street and beyond. There were thousands dancing in line round London that night. We stood outside Buckingham Palace, where the Royal Family made many appearances on the balcony; they must have been worn out. We then went to a different part of London where we saw two women wrestling topless in mud in the street. It seemed like an impromptu thing, the mud made with soil that had been dragged off flowerbeds. Taxis were creeping by; the driver made invisible by hordes of people inside the cab, clinging to its sides or on top."

By Christmas 1945 Ron was in the RAF, serving under Duration of Present Emergencies: *"I think being in the services made me grow up fast. When I was demobbed I lived on a farm at Fairlight where my parents were employed. It was very difficult to find work so I laboured on the farm for a while. I finally got a steady job at Brigg's Motor Bodies at Dagenham. Nearly all the men who worked there were ex-service and this created a strong camaraderie. We were like a band of brothers and not the type of workforce to take any bull from management; especially when the Americans took over the company."*

Ron believes that some of today's animosity towards America springs from the war years: *"While some saw the USA as our saviour in WWII, I think that America had been jealous of Britain's empire, its power and navy, for years. When WWII started they just stood back and let the Germans do the job they would have liked to have done. They only came into the war after Pearl Harbour for their own sake."* In many quarters this was a popularly held view by Britons during the war; it was more than mere envy that promoted the view of the GIs stationed in their country as being, "Over-sexed, over-paid and over here":

"Many years after the war my wife, Phyllis, and I went on a coach trip to France. We met an old army officer who shared my interest in photography. We got chatting with him and his wife and talk turned to the war and VE Night. His wife said that she had been in the Savoy Hotel, Park Lane that night and the party goers had run to the window to watch that huge conga line pass by. Odd how stories come full circle, it often happens to me. Maybe it's because, as people tell me, I'm a good listener."

Mary Perry

Mary spent her village childhood in the line of fire

Mary Perry was a vicar's daughter and at the outbreak of WWII she was living with her family in the village of Shorne, near Gravesend in Kent: *"At the start of it I had little idea of the meaning of war. I knew that I was to be evacuated and was going abroad on the ship The 'City of Benares' but that plan was changed because I had impetigo. I was evacuated to Exmouth instead, a decision that probably saved my life."*

A contemporary report of the sinking of the "City of Benares" confirms Mary's supposition: *"On Friday, September 13, 1940, the City of Benares sailed from Liverpool in a convoy of nineteen ships bound for Canada. She carried 406 crew and passengers, including 101 adults and 90 children being evacuated to Canada by the Children's Overseas Reception Board. Four days and 600 miles out to sea and shortly after 10pm, the City of Benares was torpedoed by a U-boat. The order to abandon ship was given but due to rough conditions and force 5 winds, lowering the boats was difficult and several capsized. Two hundred and forty five lives were lost either from drowning or exposure. Rescue did not reach the survivors until*

2.15pm the following afternoon, when HMS Hurricane arrived on the scene and rescued 105 people. Only 13 of the children survived, 6 of whom spent seven days in a life boat before being rescued by HMS Anthony. The Evacuation Overseas Scheme was eventually abandoned; one positive result of the tragedy was the decision to have all convoys accompanied by rescue escorts."

Mary returned home from Exmouth in time for the onslaught of the V1 and V2 raids. She lived on a hill overlooking the Thames Basin and often saw the oil refineries on fire after raids. Enemy aircraft crashed on the Gravesend Marshes and it would be her father's grim duty to conduct funeral services for the German flyers. Mary said that she cannot remember many details of VE Day: *"I do recall that we and the villagers ran up a hill, topped by a windmill, which still had its sails. We sang, danced, shouted and cheered; after dark we could see the glow of victory bonfires in the surrounding villages below. We later had a victory party. It was held in the village hall and, as vicar's wife, my mother was very involved. We had a concert and choir from a catholic school at Gravesend came to help us out with more voices. We sung 'I Vow to Thee my Country', 'Jerusalem' and a patriotic song set to Elgar's 'Pomp and Circumstance March.' I recited Thomas Hood's 'I Remember' and my sister played a piano duet with her friend. The war ruined my education and I failed my exams. But I joined the Women's Land Army, which continued to function for some years after the war, as many men had not returned to agricultural work or were not fit to do so. I thought it was a wonderful life."*

Michael Bristow-Smith

Michael (right) and his younger brother, Robin

Michael Bristow-Smith takes us back in memory to Tunbridge Wells, August 1945. VE-Day was two months past and it was a fine afternoon for the vicarage garden party. *"Things are getting back to normal perhaps, though there are still the Japs to finish off. No more doodlebugs or rockets at any rate and next week we are off to the seaside at Hastings for our first post-war holiday. In the middle of the garden party the vicar calls for quiet; he has a special announcement to make. It is about something called an atomic bomb and it sends shivers down my spine, though I don't really understand it. They say it could shorten the war against Japan. Next week comes and we travel down to Hastings by train. (Few people own a car and, anyway, there is little petrol to be had, even for essential use.) On the journey there is myself, nearly 12, my ten year old brother Robin and our fox terrier, Peter. Coping with it all, overseeing the luggage, the emergency* rations cards, the tickets and catching the train, Mother. Father is with the Royal Engineers in Africa.

It is raining on the journey down and we stop at all stations. Frant, Wadhurst, Ticehurst Road; a string of names which, except for the last, are destined in later years to become as familiar to me as my own. At Robertsbridge a diminutive and very dirty engine pants and puffs in the bay platform; the decrepit Kent and East Sussex Railway is still fiercely independent. The train slows for the curves at West St Leonards, negotiates the two tunnels and, in a hissing cloud of steam, pulls gently into shabby Hastings Station. Everything is shabby after six years of war. Eventually, Mother somehow gets us to Stonefield Terrace to be welcomed by relatives we haven't seen for some long time. Stonefield Road runs parallel with Queens Road; piled up behind it are the terraces of the West Hill, looming over the house where we are staying. Somehow, they seen threatening and I can see them tottering, crumbling and sliding down to bury us all at the bottom of the hill. But I soon forget about it. What do I remember about that holiday? At a distance of 65 years I have no coherent picture, only snapshots of memory, Most of all I remember the devastation. (Tunbridge Wells had got off lightly when it came to bomb damage.) In my mind's eye I can still see the cleared bomb sites, especially Castle Street and the seafront where Argos now stands. It seems to me that children had more freedom in those days and my brother and I were able to roam freely, without fear of traffic; there wasn't much anyway. Of course, we were with adults much of the time but we were off on our own as well, exploring twittens, alleys and mysterious flights of steps, which climbed up through the terraces, towards the green hilltop and Hastings Castle. The beach had been open since the previous summer and we were not too old to enjoy building sand-castles at low tide. I remember, too, being on the beach at high tide somewhere near Splash Point, trying unsuccessfully to dodge a wave and getting soaked for my pains. That earned me a stern rebuke from a policeman who had seen what had happened from the promenade. Our dog was soaked as well but he didn't seem to mind!

Alexandra Park was another attraction and a change from the beach. We went on the boats which had returned to the lake. In our explorations I can recall penetrating the woodland part of the park to Buckshole reservoir but I am sure we did not get as far as the Old Roar Stream. Hastings and St Leonards were full of cinemas in those pre-television days and from the gallery of the De Luxe we saw a cartoon version of " Gulliver's Travels" *while, more memorably, we went to see " Meet Me In St Louis" on pre-release, at the Gaiety Cinema in Queen's Road. We liked this film so much we saw it again at home when it was on general release. Did we go to the Marina Bathing Pool or the White Rock Swimming Baths? I can't remember but we were keen swimmers, so possibly. Odd fragments of memory surface; trolleybuses, including the old single-decker in Queen's Road, iron railings surrounding the now sadly lost town centre cricket ground, and, always, the scars of war.*

I suppose we kept an ear out to the news of war from the Far East but it would have been in the expectation of victory. No country could stand up against the new terrible weapon and, sure enough, Japan's surrender was announced, it was VJ-Day, 15th August. There was a huge bonfire on the West Hill that night with crowds milling around. Was there dancing? I think so but mostly I can still see a German helmet, stuck on a pole, in the middle of the flames. (It was all less spectacular than my Father's VJ-night when he, a Warrant Officer First Class, no less, told me many years later that the last thing he remembered was being on the roof of the Sergeant's Mess, brandishing a fire hose and singing 'The Red Flag'. He would be coming home and not going to the Far East after all.) Then the holiday was over and it was back to Tunbridge Wells and, hopefully, to the beginnings of a return to normality. Fortunately, we could not see the arid years of austerity ahead. Of course, there were more visits to Hastings, sometimes by train, sometimes by bicycle and, in later years, by car. The pull of the town was strong; I had come to dream of living there. Well, dreams sometimes do come true and forty years on, in 1985, circumstances moved me to St Leonards. I do not propose to leave. But often, as I walk through today's very different town, my mind goes back to childhood, when the traumas of the war were still fresh and I see again the desolate empty spaces that took so many years to fill."

Margaret Ball

Margaret with her mother and father

Margaret Ball was born in Highgate, London in September 1940; her father, Richard Bruder, was serving overseas with the army when the flat was bombed, the night after Maggie's birth. Her mother worked on Euston Station in the railway Lost and Found department and at the age of 9 months Maggie was sent to live with the Sisters of Charity, in a convent in Happy Valley, Clifton, near Bristol. Margaret's grandmother had been taken into the convent as a foundling and her daughter Dorothy had also been schooled there from aged 5 to 14, due to her parents' divorce. Bristol was badly bombed during the early part of the war but the convent offered a secluded, one might say isolated, life. Mrs Bruder visited her baby as often as she was able but as a small child, Margaret's main one-to-one contact was with a Sister Kathleen, of whom she has no clear recollection; neither has she of any aspects of convent life. As she spoke about her early years, a buried memory surfaced: *"I recall hearing the air-raid warnings as I lay in bed at the convent and I would wriggle my head from side to side, in an attempt to drown out the frightening sound. I continued this habit after the war and on my return with my mother to London, which was during the late spring or early summer of 1945. My life at the convent had been so quiet and tranquil that I found the noise and bustle of the railway station and steam trains terrifying. By then my mother was living in a flat in Balham, in South West*

London, overlooking Nightingale Square; locals said the nightingales did sing there at one time."

Margaret went to the Holy Ghost Catholic Primary School. She had to walk through streets that had been badly bombed when on her way to another school for lunchtime, as the Roman Catholic School she attended did not cater for school meals. In some areas the rubble of the ruined houses had not even been cleared away. Maggie spoke of talking to prisoners of war in the area: *"I can't say if the prisoners were German or Italian or why they were there. I do remember when my father was demobilised and came home. I found this difficult, as he was a stranger to me and up until then I had enjoyed my mother's undivided attention. My father has been fighting in Italy, in the Battle of the River Po Valley; in later years my mother said that he went away to war a happy innocent and came home a different man. He would never talk of the war. Along with everyone else post war, we suffered the privations of austerity. The food was poor; things I particularly remember disliking were spam fritters, dried egg and toad-in-the-hole. An aunt in America would sometimes send us parcels; I recall things in those parcels I had never seen before; jello and milk shake. One parcel contained a wonderful dress for me, appliquéd with tulips. One of my father's many cousins in Ireland would sometimes send us the Catholic Herald interleaved with rashers of bacon and we had big fry-ups. In 1947, two years after my father's return from the front, my sister Katie was born. It was only in middle age that I began to realise how my earlier years had affected me quite deeply, in that I felt I was an outsider looking in. I now wonder if, although never spoken of, a fellow kinship was what drew me to the man I married. He had been sent to an orphanage, after his mother was killed during the bombing, and did not experience the bonding between a mother and a child during his formative years."*

Keith Cook

Keith Cook, aged 18

During a pre-WWII visit to Gatwick as a child, Keith Cook saw a German airliner; its presence led to an ominous-sounding discussion between the adults, which he did not understand. Some time later, again pre-war, he was in the outpatients department of the Royal East Sussex Hospital in Hastings, when someone called out that a Zeppelin was approaching. Everyone rushed outside and somebody said, *"Did you see them waving to us?"* His family had similar experiences at home in Priory Avenue and there was talk about these so-called friendly flights being used to take photographs.

"After the war was declared I watched the air raid shelters being dug out by a Ruston Bucyrus Excavator at the foot of Torfield, at the bottom of Old London Road; in post-war years our gang used to play in them. During the phoney war I feel sure that we took in a couple of evacuees for a short time

but they were soon moved away, when it was realised that Hastings had become part of the war front line, with barbed wire and steel fortifications along the promenade and sea shore. My next prominent memory is of being evacuated on 12th July, 1940; of going to Clive Vale School carrying a suitcase and gas mask, being put aboard a Maidstone and District bus and taken to Hastings Railway Station. A few children were crying but most of us laughed, seeing this as a big adventure. After a train journey to Harpenden we were feeling tired and hungry and no longer adventurous. On being told by my kindly billetors to write a safe-arrival card to my parents, I asked. "Are we allowed to say where we are?" Secrecy and security were already part of my mindset. There was a hostel there for Hastings children with health problems, of which I was one. I was eventually fit enough to be billeted with a family".

Some time later Keith was joined in Harpenden by his mother, following a frightening experience she had whilst cleaning windows at home. The blast from a tip and run raider's bomb had almost blown her out of the window into the basement several feet below. *"Dad was left on his own in Hastings, his only companion the family cat. After my father's day time duties he would return home and cook his lonely meal, change into his Home Guard uniform and with his Browning automatic rifle, patrol the railway line single-handedly from Ore Station to the Queen's Road railway bridge. The rifle, issued to Dad's Home Guard Unit, was so rusty on delivery that the Commanding Officer was going to return it as unserviceable but my Dad, the son of a gamekeeper, made it an excellent weapon again. He was rewarded with having it allocated to him. One night, early in the war, Dad saw a great orange glow from across the Channel. It proved to be from the Dunkirk evacuation. Months later we learned that a couple of our soldiers had been held back to set light to our fuel dumps, one of them was my Dad's brother, Colin; he got home safely. My father was machine-gunned when returning on foot from Glyne Gap sidings to Hastings station; he managed to hide at a line-side hut until the attacker gave up the game. Dad was not called up as he was a railway worker and the railway system was an important part of the war effort; his job was classified as a reserved occupation. Rail workers had to wear an oval-shaped badge to signify this, especially important if they wished to move in and out of areas restricted under wartime regulations, such as the south coast. My mother returned to Hastings later in the war and I was left behind in Harpenden, spending anxious days without letters; postal services were often delayed by bombing raids. Despite the air raids, most of us evacuees would go back to our* family for school holidays. When at home my sleep was often disturbed by raids and I have recollections of being dragged from bed in the middle of the night and pushed into the Morrison shelter in our downstairs dining room. During one of my wartime visits to Hastings we went down to Pebsham, a one-time airfield, to see where a Liberator bomber had made a forced landing; it had ended up at the bottom of somebody's garden in Bexhill Road.

We boys used to pride ourselves on aircraft identification but my skills failed me when my mother and I were in our garden; we heard what I believed to be the familiar engine-roar and whistle of a Spitfire, not far away. "Good Old Spit," we mistakenly cried. This was followed by an explosion; I believe it was a bomb that was dropped on Havelock Road. (In 1968 I was walking along the Ridge when I heard the familiar aircraft roar and whistle; instinct said, "Spitfire", reason said it could not be. On my return home I heard the sounds again. There was indeed a Spit, pursuing a German aircraft, an ME 109. It was a sequence being shot for the film "Battle of Britain.") In the period of the doodlebugs my parents and I would sometimes go up to the West Hill in the hope of seeing the big guns in action. On one occasion a doodlebug was approaching Hastings, when an artillery shot tilted the missile and it plunged towards a small Royal Navy ship, anchored off Rock-a-Nore. We looked on in horror but the doodlebug mercifully missed the vessel. The ship up-anchored and cruised around, presumably to give the crew a chance to pick up some of the stunned fish for their supper. My mother and I had another doodlebug experience some time later: We were standing outside our open kitchen door when a V1 came over the East Hill. The guns hit it, creating a huge explosion. We cheered then looked at each other in amazement; we were still standing together but inside the kitchen. The blast had lifted us through the open doorway but we had not even felt it.

In December 1944, our school returned from evacuation by special train, via a circuitous route; I still have my pencilled log of that journey. In 1945, my parents and I went up to London for the VE Day celebrations and became part of the crowd outside Buckingham Place, chanting, "We want the King!" In due course, and to loud acclamation he appeared on the balcony, with the royal family and Winston Churchill. My parents decided it was wise to return home early; everyone else must have decided likewise. Walking in that massive crowd was like being carried along by in a river; the next moment we saw my father lifted off his feet and carried away helplessly from us, down the steps of a nearby Tube Station. We shouted to policeman who *was trying to control the crowds, "He doesn't want to go down there, get him out!" Incredibly, the officer managed to clear a way for Dad to get up the steps. Dad was too exhausted to even bend down to pick up his trilby hat, which had got knocked off. On another visit to London we passed a Spitfire on display and my mother kissed it on the engine cowling, saying that if ever she got the chance to kiss a Spitfire she would do it. Victory celebrations in Hastings included a triumphal visit to Hastings by Field Marshall Montgomery. I painted several union flags and displayed them in our upstairs windows, only to see Monty sweep past us and the nearby school at speed.*

After the war the German prisoners of war put on a concert at what was then called the Robertson Street Congregational Church. The POWs came from Normanhurst, where they were agricultural workers. Far from feeling animosity we regarded them with sympathy and the concert created a lovely atmosphere. This must have meant so much to these men, who were now wondering when they would return to what remained of their homes. As a boy I was a keen train spotter and made a note of my oddest "cop" on the 8th June 1946, when I saw a 72220 WD (War Department) diesel loco at Kennington Oval, in the mechanised column of the London Victory Parade; thus commemorating that the railways played a vital part in the war both at home and abroad." Keith served in the Royal Air Force from 1949 to 1951. After demobilisation he was employed in the newly formed National Health Service followed by several years as Registrar of Births and Deaths, with subsequent qualifications he broadened his career path. Nearing retirement, he returned to the post of Registrar, to give him more time for his family, interests and community involvement.

Monica Hoad

Monica enjoying life on the land

Monica Hoad, too young for the Land Army during the war, became an agricultural worker. She recorded her reflections on war, victory and the years following in a memoir for her family, from which the following is an extract.

"As our armies progressed in Europe life on the home front became less hazardous and by May 1945 the war was over. I actually heard the news

from my friend; she came rushing into the cowshed that I was spring cleaning, standing on the rafters and white-washing them. She shouted, 'It's all over, the war's over!' Everywhere there was a sense of relief and people tried to arrange parties wherever possible. Of course the Far Eastern War was not over until August, when the two atom bombs were dropped on Hiroshima and Nagasaki. The farm where I worked in Westfield was sold in October 1945 and I was sorry to be leaving, but the Women's Land Army would take me then as I was 17 years old. I was delighted when I was accepted as a member, after an initial interview in Lewes and a medical in Hastings. My uniform soon followed, three enormous parcels, I had never had so many new clothes at once and all were of good quality. I thought I had all my birthdays and Christmases, all rolled into one. Early in November I was posted to a small but exceedingly well-run farm on the borders of Sussex and Kent. There was a herd of Guernsey cows producing lovely creamy milk. I was really happy working on that particular farm. I liked my employers and the mature man I worked alongside was one those countrymen full of knowledge and expertise, his skills seemed endless. I felt a sense of satisfaction working on this farm; I had excellent lodgings with a middle-aged couple, lovely food and a warm and comfy home. In my second year there, with the war well and truly over, German prisoners were employed as labourers. We had two very nice chaps; one called George came and looked after the horses and the other, Richard, a nice man, made himself cosy in the loft of one of the outbuildings. In Germany he had owned a hardware business. His wife and family were able to keep in touch with him and the farmer's wife would provide Richard with a few goodies to send home, as they were suffering quite badly in Germany. Those Germans remaining in the camps were very resourceful; they would make toys out of scraps of wood, mostly planes, trains or lorries. Brightly painted, these sold well, as toys were not that plentiful. I can remember buying some for my young stepbrothers. One trick the Germans had was to split matchsticks in half with a razor so that they got 100 from a box of 50.

After two years, longing for more work experience, I answered an advert for relief milkers but it was a sad mistake. I went to many farms afterwards but none ever came up to my lovely little Guernsey herd and the nice family I had left. I gave up relief milking after an accident. I was mounting a large Shire horse and I grabbed its mane, as I had done loads of times before and made a leap. I slipped and dislocated my shoulder and was left with a partially paralysed hand. I next took a job, still in the WLA, as a dairymaid in Berkshire on an estate of landed gentry. It was a beautiful place; I had my own flat above the dairy, which had a washing and sterilising room, a butter making room and a show dairy. Next door was where the cowman and his wife had lived before the war. My employers had big house parties and they had shaken hands not only with our royalty but also foreign royalty and dignitaries. My job was doing the milking and serving fresh milk to the villagers who came between 7.30-8.00am; I had about 50 customers. I also had to take the money and deal with accounts. A lady came to teach me how to make butter for the big house but I only did that for short while. The flat was so nice and to have my independence was lovely.

I was 20 when I took on this job and I had young man, who wished to become serious. Up to then marriage was not on my agenda; I had a love affair with farming and didn't want anything to interfere with this. The estate or village was rather like a big family. A year prior to my going there the lady owner had died, everyone spoke so kindly of her saying she would visit the sick in hospital and take a genuine interest in their welfare but with new owners and progress, things changed." Monica married her "young man", an agricultural worker. She gave up farm work and had nine children and, over the years, she became the cherished matriarch to a large extended family. She died in May 2009 and is buried in a rural cemetery, bordered by the open countryside that she loved.

Conifer Rowland

Conifer in France towards the end of World War Two

Conifer Rowland was born in the Yorkshire Dales in January 1918 and at the age of seventeen, after being educated at boarding school, went to the girls' Lycée in Rennes, France. When she was nineteen she met and married a French man, Pierre Canneva, and settled down to French provincial life. Pierre joined the French army as soon as war was declared in 1939 and was subsequently taken prisoner when the Germans invaded France. Conifer escaped to England with her baby daughter and the couple did not meet again until after the war. WWII changed the expected path of Conifer's life completely. She recounted how she returned to her parents' home in Yorkshire after escaping from France in 1940:

"One morning, when I had been home about a month, my father looked up over the top of his Times, 'There's a French chap called de Gaulle starting a Free French Movement in London. Write to him today and see if you can join.' I don't remember a thing about any correspondence or question of an interview, but in no time I was on the train to London, where I would stay, to begin with, with friends. The very next morning I was walking down Gordon Street in Bloomsbury to the Hospital for Tropical Diseases, where I was to report to the Free French. And so began four years of undreamed of independence, the camaraderie of the forces, the excitement of wartime London, and then the return to France with the Red Cross after D-Day; years of independence which, like for so many people of my age, were to prove so unsettling as to make a return to pre-war life impossible, pointing my life in a direction I could not possibly have foreseen on the day I walked into the Hospital for Tropical Diseases. I spent four years at the Free French General Headquarters in London, and then joined a small contingent of the Free French Red Cross. After the Allied invasion we were sent to France where, with my friend Piu, I drove a truck delivering medicines to various Red Cross bases around the country."

In December 1944 the war in Europe was clearly in its final phase; the Russians were closing in on Germany from the East and other allies pushing inexorably from the West. *"Just before Christmas, Commandant Morin, head of the Free French Red Cross, my friend Piu and I, with our truck full of boxes of medicines, set off for the South of France. I was the only one who could drive; the journey took three days along roads damaged by the American Army as it had raced north to liberate Paris. Unlike the richer regions of the north of France, where, at a price, food was available, the situation south of Lyon was desperate. We spent the night in a small hotel where, with beans and cigarettes, worth more than gold as barter and which Morin had brought from England, he persuaded the inn-keeper to kill and cook a turkey, boil some large onions, the only vegetable available, and give us a round loaf of the rather sour peasant bread. No butter of course. This bounty would sustain us for the next three days.*

Driving down the mountains to the Mediterranean, surely one of the loveliest approaches in the world, we arrived in Cannes in the late afternoon. It was a small town in those days. We had all three known it before the war, Morin having once lived there, Piu had a house in Antibes and I had spent part of my honeymoon nearby. There were no means of communication, but we were confident of finding a good hotel and at least of having a hot bath. Nothing had prepared us for the result of the allied landings five months earlier. All the hotels were closed and shuttered and there was an air of desolation everywhere. The manager of the Hotel Miramar on the Croisette opened up three rooms for us; there was no heating, no hot water, no food and no service! Huddled in blankets in Morin's room, eating our turkey, cold onions and horrible bread, he said to me, 'Tomorrow morning, after we have delivered the boxes, we'll drop Piu off in Antibes to see about her house, and you and I will go and see Picasso.' I had never heard of Picasso! There was no mass media in those days. Modern Art had not penetrated my Yorkshire boarding school or my small circle of friends.

On a perfect, still Mediterranean winter's day, leaving Piu in the square in Antibes, I drove up the hair-raising winding road to Saint Paul de Vence, through the medieval arch and pulled up in front of the famous Hotel de la Colombe d'Or. Picasso came out to greet Morin with open arms. He seemed pleased with the few slices of cold turkey I handed him in a paper bag. He was a little, brown nut of a man, bald on the front and top of his head, with the hair at the back and sides much longer than in the photographs we have become used to seeing. He had dark, piercing eyes and, for his age, a very wrinkled skin. He wore khaki shorts and shirt, with brown leather sandals on his bare feet. His voice was deep with a very strong Spanish accent. Putting his arm tightly round my waist, he took us into a long, narrow room with a wall of windows overlooking the spectacular view down to the sea. He insisted on my sitting close to him, much too close, on a small wooden bench. While he and Morin caught up with news of the last four years, I looked around the room and received my initiation into the world of modern art. There were pictures everywhere, by Matisse and other contemporary painters, all completely incomprehensible to my untutored eye. The garish colours, the grotesque facial expressions, the bodily distortions left me utterly bemused. I learned later that he was loath to part with any of his work (except in return for money) but when, mercifully, it was time to leave, he took a piece of paper, drew a few quick lines, wrote 'La Belle Anglaise', signed it 'Picasso', added the date and handed it to me. A few days later I found it in my bag. What rubbish, I thought. It doesn't look a bit like me. I threw it away!

It is strange how selective, in old age, memory can be. Driving my truck round France delivering medicines was one of the highlights of my life. I loved every minute of it, and yet the details of those days are blurred. Where did I get the petrol and the jerry cans filled? Where did we get our food? After a while I was mostly on my own. I do remember going to Tours by myself, spending two days with an American unit; I wonder why? I stayed in a good hotel but had my meals with the Americans. The food was awful! Tinned corn and jam with meat at every meal. In the particularly hard winter of 1944/45 there was deep snow and ice. In between journeys I would return to Paris, and was there for Christmas. Early in the New Year I drove to the South of France, again with Morin and Piu, with the last boxes of medicine. On our return to Paris the unit was closed down and we were demobbed and I had to leave my truck at an Army Depot. It broke my heart. Piu went back to London and I was seconded to the British Red Cross, whose offices were in the British Embassy in the Faubourg St. Honore. The man at the head of this was the theatre impresario, Val Gielgud (brother of John) and I became his personal driver. It was a dream job. Paris was achingly beautiful that spring. I had, by this time, many friends, both French and American, and was invited out every night. I remember a flat in the Avenue Montaigne, sitting on the floor listening to Sacha Guitry telling me anecdotes of his life, his voice as mesmeric as on the stage. There was lunch with Maurice Chevalier at his beautiful house outside Paris, an unforgettable evening with a Russian count and his many relations, all émigrés, living in Paris since the Revolution, who made us weep with laughter as he told terrible Russian tragedies in his deep, dramatic voice. I attended a reception at the Canadian Embassy and a lunch at one of the most beautiful old houses in the Boulevard St.Germain, with a footman behind each guest. There was an atmosphere of euphoria; the allies were closing in on Berlin. Then on 8th May it was over. That night we joined a crowd of many thousands walking from the Arc de Triomphe, down the Champs Elysees to the Place de la Concorde. It was strange; there was no singing or dancing as there was in London. It was a quiet, subdued crowd as if the five terrible years of enemy occupation had taken their toll and left them exhausted and just quietly thankful that it was all over."

Some years after the war ended, Conifer divorced and re-married. She travelled the world with her new husband until he suddenly died when she was 52. After an exciting and eventful life, Conifer died on 25th August 2009 at the age of 91. On June 18th 2010 Conifer's daughter, Paddy Manning, was invited to a ceremony in the French village Batz-sur-Mer, to mark the 70th anniversary of Charles de Gaulle's call, after the capitulation of the French Government to the Nazis in 1940, to all free French men and women, to join him in London. Paddy said: *"The invitation was extended to me to lend a more personal element, particularly as my mother was an English girl; the ceremony was extremely moving. For the occasion I also mounted an exhibition in the local town hall of copies of documents I had found in my mother's papers that related to her five years in the Free French."*

Deeday White

DeeDay in his Hastings Old Town antique shop

Deeday White, a lifelong resident of Hastings Old Town and one of nature's entrepreneurs, was born in 1944. He has become famous locally and in the wider world for his unusual name. Sitting in his antique shop, amid the bustle that typifies his working life, he talked about his memories and the origin of his unique name.

"My father, Albert George White, has three sons, Bertie, Kenny and myself. Bertie and my father were fishermen and crewed on the Hastings Lifeboat; Kenny took up engineering. In the war my father was in a reserved occupation as he was both fisherman and lifeboat man. When I was expected, my father put up a list in The Royal Standard Pub, to invite suggestions for a name for the new baby. I was born on 6th June 1944 so the top suggestion was D-Day, the code name for the invasion of occupied Europe. Two days later my Dad went to register the birth of his son with the

name as D-Day. The registrar said that name could not be used, as it was a military secret. So my father showed him the newspaper headlines, 'Second Day of D-Day', and asked him how much of a secret is that? However, he compromised by putting double e in Deeday and the registrar accepted it. HMS Rodney was one of the first boats to open up the D-Day bombardment, hence my middle name of Rodney. I have seen many changes in the Old Town. I can remember pushing my Mum's washing in a pram to the wash house and going in for a bath. It cost three old pennies, four if two people shared; a Mr Casper oversaw the baths. The wash house was about 60 feet long and had a row of deep sinks; working side-by-side, the women would exchange all the local gossip as they scrubbed and I'm sure the reason our washing was so bright was because my Mum used to go to the wash house more often than she needed, to catch up on the latest scandal! I played football in The Bourne and tore down Pollard Hill in go-carts. There were four bomb craters on the East Hill between Tackleway and the East Hill lift, in which me and my mates made camps; we collected wood and lino from the beach to roof them in. We were able to sleep all night in them with no worries. A favourite lark was to build a grate and chimney in the wall of the crater and put balls of earth to cook in a fire. When the balls were really hard we had fights with them. We called the game 'make and bake, chuck and duck.' We boys also used to play in the WWII pill boxes at Rock-A-Nore and in the caves in the cliff, which had been used by the army. One of these we called the Iron Cave because the army had installed an iron door at its entrance. The army also made steps to get up the caves; they are still there now but overgrown with brambles. There is a rock up there shaped like an upside down elephant's foot, next to one of the pill boxes; we called it 'Elephant's Foot Rock.' It had an iron bar set in it and in the war there was a machine gun mounted on it. The area along the cliffs near Rock-a-Nore, called the Govers, dips down to sea level and in the war it was seen as potential landing site for a German invasion, so it was encircled by barbed wire and heavily mined. I remember the army coming down after the war to clear the area and blowing up the mines, which us kids would go and watch. Me and two pals took part in a public information film; we had to act out picking up a mine under a hedge, it was disarmed of course, to warn kids of the dangers of handing objects that were laying about the place. At Fairlight Quarry there was a WWII building that is still there now, there was also a set of firing butts and a target range, which consisted of a huge, man-made bank with the target in front of it. After the war, as kids we would dig into this and find the spent bullets and go home with pocketfuls. The bank is all grown over with grass now but where that is cut into with paths I'm sure you could still dig out bullets to this day. We made our own entertainment in those days; there was no TV then to keep us amused. On the East Hill was our swing tree, which had a high, overhanging branch; the boys used to go down to the beach and steal a length of rope and sling it over the branch to make a swing that would last all summer. I remember that David (Ickle) Joy was the best tree climber. The swing tree was a gathering place for the local youngsters, the boys showing off their climbing and swinging skills to the girls. The council eventually cut off the branch of the tree, as our exploits were considered dangerous.

At three years old I went to school at little All Saints; the school was two doors down from The Cinque Ports Pub. In the basement was a kitchen where they cooked the school dinners. On a sunny day, if you were good, you took a fold-up bed to the playground and if you went to sleep, you were given a sweet on waking. The school has since been demolished and a block of flats stands on the site. From All Saints I went to Clive Vale School. I was given one shilling (twelve old pennies, five new pence) per day; nine pennies were for dinner, two pennies for bus journeys and one to spend. I walked both ways so I had 3d to spend or save. I can remember saving 240 pennies and changing it for my very own pound; a real note that I could fold, just like my Dad did! I left school at 14 and went fishing but it was not for me, it was too cold, too wet, too smelly and too unreliable. I started working in the building trade and bought the last of the slum properties in the Old Town. They had no water, heating or bathrooms and only outside toilets. I have owned over 30 properties in Hastings Old Town and now I live only 200 yards from the house I was born in. My father and brothers were members of the Winkle Club and I was enrolled too. I married at the age of 21 and Number two, Old Humphrey Avenue, (formerly owned by the president of the Winkle Club), was ours for the grand sum of £1,500. In 2001 the value of this house was £140,000. This property became the subject of some comment when I painted it battle-ship grey and put barbed wire on the window sills. I painted the name Stalag II over the door and a swastika on the gate. My front gate was removed and used as evidence in court. In 1968 I found myself in possession of an illegal gun and attracted the interest of the law. Growing up with a name like mine had good and bad points but I always liked talking to people about their wartime experiences. I began building a vast collection of military items and even while still at school I would buy, sell and trade."

On the 50th anniversary of the D-Day Invasion in 1994, Deeday went to France with a German friend, staying with a French family, to join in the international events to mark the occasion. In 2009 he made as trip to Omaha Beach and the nearby town of St Mere Eglise. The town played a significant part in the World War II Normandy landings because it stood right in the middle of route N13, which the Germans would have probably used on any counterattack on the troops landing on Utah and Omaha Beaches. In the early morning of 6th June 1944, two US units occupied the town, making it one of the first places to be liberated. A now famous incident in the liberation involved US paratrooper, John Steele, whose parachute caught on the spire of the town church; all he could do was watch the fighting going on below. He hung on the spire for two hours, pretending to be dead, after which the Germans took him prisoner. Steele later escaped and rejoined his division. It happened that Deeday's visit to St Mere Eglise coincided with that of a US veteran, who was signing copies of a book he had written about the invasion. When the writer met Deeday and heard his name he got him sign the books too. French TV conducted two interviews with him over his fortnight stay. On being asked if he thought that having such an unusual name had opened doors for him Deeday said it had, literally, on a visit he made to the D-Day Museum at Arromanches. He was about to be photographed on the steps of the town's commemorative museum, between the signs on either side of the entrance that declared, "D-Day Museum", when an attendant opened the door. On learning the reason for the photo he looked at Deeday's passport, and then invited him to sign the visitor's book and to visit the museum free of charge any time he wished. Deeday says that his name has never bothered him; that the Old Town is full of nick-names but he was given his at birth. He has even had post correctly delivered that was addressed merely "Deeday, Hastings Old Town." The name is set to be carried on: *"When my son was born what else could I do but call him Deeday? He joined the army and instead of being called "Chalky"; as men called White usually are, he had a nick-name ready made: It was looked upon by his mates as an honour rather than a cause for leg-pulling."*

Don Samways

The young Don Samways on parade

When peace came Don was living in Bognor Regis. He and his parents had moved there in late 1944 from the Black Country, where Don had spent his first 12 years. His parents wanted a better life, away from the factory chimneys and grime, and when the south coast was again opened up after being off-limits throughout the war, they took the opportunity to join relatives. Don said that as war ended he remembers little of his new home:

"Being at the seaside and living 200 yards from the beach was so wildly different from Walsall and Birmingham that the great change to peacetime was less significant. But one vivid memory was when, as if to celebrate the war's end, a mine washed ashore at the end of our road and blew out many of our windows, something that we'd been lucky to avoid in all the years of Midlands air raids. Bognor was returning to life, even if the beach was still out of bounds the holidaymakers started to arrive, a summer variety show called Dazzle and small seaside businesses opened. On the train to school at

Chichester, we passed huge airfields like Tangmere and Ford, where, as soon as the war finished, thousands of fighters and bombers were standing unemployed. At school, however, I was regarded as a foreigner, my strange Brummie accent was thought by some to be German; at best I was thought of as a refugee, to be mistrusted and disliked and I returned this feeling with vigour. It was not my finest hour and I was heartily glad when I moved to Hastings in 1947.

In Birmingham I 'had a good war', and my memories of that time are much more vivid than those of the Bognor days. As Chamberlain gave us the news on 3rd September I was rushing up and down our garden in Coronation Road in short-trousered excitement and waiting for the bombs to rain down, as were the men folk of our road, albeit in longer trousers. So carried away were they that they started to dig a deep trench as a communal air raid shelter in the field behind our houses. The shelter was never finished or even properly dug but we kids happily used it for our war games. The bombs never did rain down on our road, although there were some anxious moments and near misses. Anderson shelters were provided and we were to spend many nights in them in the next year or two. It was hard going for my parents, especially my Dad who, too old for the Forces, worked like a dog every day building Spitfires in the vast factory nearby, then came home to become an Air Raid Warden at night. How he did it for so long, I don't know but there was certainly a great spirit abroad in those days as just about everyone did his bit. I have to admit I found the war exciting and fun. I followed the news avidly, and was allowed by my kind parents to subscribe to 'The War Illustrated', a magazine which I took throughout the war. I also amassed a fine collection of shrapnel from the anti-aircraft gunfire and the odd bomb, rushing out into the street in the early morning after every air raid to collect the best pieces. We kids had great freedom on which the war didn't seem to impinge. In 1942, and 10 years old, I became a keen collector of engine numbers, first at the important railway junction two or three miles away, but then, wanting more variety, I travelled over the railway system, like thousands of other spotters, with total freedom. In school caps and mostly still in short trousers, we wandered around stations, clambered about engine sheds, even ventured into locomotive works. All of this was trespassing of course but rarely were we shouted at or chased away. My parents just let me get on with it, no doubt so wrapped up in their wartime responsibilities that they didn't have time for my misadventures, as long as I survived.

Though Hastings wasn't far along the coast from Bognor, the atmosphere there seemed altogether brighter when I arrived in 1947. The town appeared thronged with visitors; the beach was open, as were the pier, the bathing pool and swimming baths; the rented bathing huts were already mostly taken. Post-war enjoyment and prosperity were well established; or so it appeared to my schoolboy understanding. I'm sure much food was still on ration and luxuries very difficult to find. I remember the mad rush there was when one shop received a supply of nylon stockings. I still needed a year or more to finish my studies, so found myself at Hastings Grammar School, located then in Nelson Road. Though far from a model, or capable, student, I quite enjoyed my last few terms of school, mainly because I made some friends, with whom I joined youth clubs and, very tentatively, began to talk to girls, also learning to dance and play tennis. The pleasures of the Robertson Street Congregational Church Young People's Society really changed my young life and these experiences no doubt coloured my favourable impression of Hastings.

This was further heightened when I joined the staff of the Hastings and St Leonards Observer in late 1948 as an apprentice reporter. Initially, at least, I was the only junior on the editorial staff, so naturally got the lowliest jobs, from making tea to covering meetings of the Baptist Missionary Society and funerals of local dignitaries; it was a good way to learn the noble art of journalism. Rather to my regret I'd missed what must have been a lively wartime at the Observer. One of the reporters who was there recalled that an anti-aircraft gun was mounted on the roof of the building, and its thunderous reports were usually the first sign that a Luftwaffe hit-and-run raider, machine guns rattling and bombs at the ready, was already swooping over the town, and it was time to dive under the desks. My-life-in-Hastings story was forcibly shortened in 1953, when I became a patient in Fairlight TB Sanatorium, then located in Ore village, where the old trolleybuses used to turn round. After a year or so there, I was more or less recovered, but the medics wouldn't allow me to return to the 'rigours' of newspaper reporting, so I was obliged to leave Hastings and never lived and worked there again. I still have relatives and friends in Hastings and happily return for regular visits; overall I have pleasurable memories of the place and its people."

Joan Holt

Joan in her Land Army days at Mountfield

Joan Holt, aged 88, was born on her father's farm in Salehurst, Robertsbridge. She joined the Land Army in 1942 and was employed on Castle Farm at nearby Mountfield. During the war Joan was photographed by the Daily Mail and a picture of her wearing a tin hat and driving a tractor appeared under the headline, "Steel Helmets for Land Girls." It was not all work as Joan remembers: *"There was a club in Robertsbridge for the Land Army members, where we could go to play darts and table tennis. It was just for the girls, no men allowed, although I am sure they would have liked to have joined."* Joan tackled all the jobs on the farm including driving a rackety old green van which had virtually no brakes. To enable her to stop, Joan kept a brick on a string on the floor of the van and when she needed to stop she would open the door, leap out and put the brick under the front wheel. She used the reverse process to get going again, keeping the brick ready for her next stop. *"Soldiers billeted in the vicinity got to know about my van with no brakes and would jump out in front of me in the hilly lanes around Robertsbridge. It would have served them right if I had run them over, but I never did."*

When asked about her wages Joan said that she thinks it was two pounds and eight shillings (£2.40) per week and she gave her mother all of that except for fifteen shillings (75p), which she kept for her own needs. Joan remembered that a pair of stocking was about a shilling (5p). *"We had a lot of doodlebugs over Robertsbridge and one crashed and exploded on the edge of Darwell Reservoir; the fragments of the rocket stayed there for years. A German plane crashed in fields in Robertsbridge, killing the pilot; my parents would not let me go and see the place. But I often rode my bike to work through air raids; I think we were more dedicated then."*

Joan would have liked to have pursued a career in forestry after the war but she married in 1947. Her husband was a forester and Joan helped him in his work, driving the lorry and tractor. One day, a few weeks after their wedding, he had to take a load of trees long distance and Joan asked if she could travel with him in the back of the lorry, sitting atop the great tree trunks: *"I was always something of a daredevil. Everything went well until we got inside the Blackwall tunnel when there was a breakdown ahead and the lorry was stuck for an hour. It was made worse for me because there was a double-decker bus on the opposite lane and the passengers could see me sitting on the trees and became concerned, much as I tried to tell them that I was fine. Of course, it would never be allowed today."* Joan said that she remembered the start of the war more clearly than its end: *"I was in Bexhill on the terrace of the De la Warr Pavilion, looking out to sea, when the news came through. I started crying because my mother was at home in Robertsbridge and I thought that the bombing would start at once; I was eighteen at the time. When victory came at last it was wonderful. We took trestles outside for a party and there was dancing in the evening; it was like a dream."* Joan, who still lives in Salehurst, is the proud bearer of the Women's Land Army and Timber Corps Medal which she was awarded in 2008.

Richard Pitcairn-Knowles

Richard with his parents and family pets in 1945

Richard Pitcairn-Knowles was born and brought up at the Riposo Health Cure Hydro on the Ridge; the hydro was founded by his grandfather in 1912. Reflecting on the end of the war, Richard commented on how strange it is that he has so many stark memories of earlier in the war: low-flying German planes with machine guns roaring, dropping bombs on Hastings, planes crashing, the blue skies and vapour trails of the Battle of Britain. He recalled cycling to the Battle Senlac Cinema in the blackout, doodle-bugs clattering overhead and sometimes exploding nearby and shattering every front window in the house, but so few moments are remembered from the days of relief when it was all over.

"My twelfth birthday occurred on 21st December 1944, so I was getting on for thirteen during the summer of 1945 and should be able to remember so much more than I do. Was it a long hot summer? One's childhood days of weather are never remembered for the periods of long dull days that must have been common, but for the pleasures of warm sun or the excitement of

snow; the 1945 summer was sunny and warm as far as I can remember. The background atmosphere of relief on VE Day and VJ Day, in May and August, must have been felt by the young as much as by the old, although I am sure that when it was over I missed the pre D-Day excitement of army convoy-watching, the massing of army lorries at the army camp in Grange Road on the Ridge and in the surrounding muddy lanes, followed by the excitement of looking up to see Dakota planes towing gliders full of troops and supplies. This seemed to go on for months, as the Allies advanced across Europe. At age eleven it was fun to cycle down Grange Road and chat to the Americans who were there for only a few days. When the war ended there were victory parties everywhere and the sun always seemed to shine on these events. I am sorry to say that only two events stand out; the celebration in the field next to St Helens Church and another near Hydneye House School, opposite to Little Ridge Farm, where the Conquest Hospital stands now. I am not sure which party came first, I think it was St Helens, probably on VE Day, and then Hydneye House on VJ Day but I am sure there were other events, as I remember winning the slow bicycle races at these, more than twice, and being just a little surprised that yet another opportunity arose to show off my simple skill. I think the Hastings Grammar School returned from evacuation during 1945 and I was soon accepted there into the second year, by then I was twelve plus. My education during the war was strange; mostly a couple of days a week by myself with the Misses Lock who were a retired teacher and her sister, at Sedlescombe. Perhaps being interviewed by the Grammar School headmaster, Mr Hyder, and the shock of being suddenly in a big school, with so many other boys, deleted my memories of the months immediately after the war."

On being asked if he thought that growing up as a wartime child influenced the person he is today, Richard said that remembering the security he felt in the war years engenders feelings of lingering guilt. He asks himself why he should have enjoyed those years when others were dying, being maimed, losing family and friends, not to mention their homes and businesses. He felt that one of the effects the war had on him was to leave him with the inability to throw away anything that one day be useful. *"We celebrate when I say to my wife that I am putting an article of clothing in the bin. I do not waste food, eating anything slightly past its use-by date instead of binning it. I like to think I am careful about money; it is not meanness but 'greenness', a matter of not being wasteful. If one can avoid two car journeys and make one cover two tasks, this is common sense. I like to think that I am self-sufficient and can look can look after myself and the family. Being an only child, when all other children in Hastings were evacuated, has had an effect I didn't notice at the time, making me self-sufficient but probably a little odd. I think this comes from being allowed the freedom to rush around on my bicycle whenever a bomb dropped or a plane crashed somewhere within a few miles. I am sure that is why I like long distance running. The sense of smell can be very evocative; if I catch a whiff of crushed leaves when trees are felled in summer, I am catapulted in memory to the crater of a doodle-bug in the woods in 1944 and am surrounded by devastated trees and picking up souvenirs. This was when the rocket blew out the windows at Riposo but I was so secure that I heard nothing and slept well. Nowadays, the nighttime drone of a distant plane jolts the question, in a half-awake moment, 'Is it one of ours or one of theirs'; until the realisation comes that we have moved on seventy years. The war years pulled people together; they exhibited politeness, no queue-jumping, putting up with whatever came along, savouring the smallest luxury. I am sad that wars continue, prejudice is still rife, the gap between rich and poor widens and, to cap it all, the world population has risen in my lifetime from 2.8 billion to 7.2 billion. 'Green' measures without birth control are useless but telling people how many children they can have is political suicide. Here my feelings of guilt come to the fore again; my wife, Pamela, and I have three children and six grandchildren! We love them very much but we could also have loved one child and one grandchild."*

Pam Eaves

Pam Eaves, still dancing in 1946, aged 13

Writer Pam Eaves remembers standing in her family's tiny garden in North London in 1944 and watching aeroplanes go over in droves; the droning noise filled the sky: *"For once, I felt safe because, 'They're ours', said our neighbour, and he was smiling. I'm not sure if what I remember next actually happened on VE day, or a little later, but I do recall prancing around on the back of a lorry all done up in fancy clothes with a lot of other little girls from our dancing school. I can't remember exactly what we were wearing, but there was a swathe of red, white and blue fluttering all along the route, as the procession of lorries slowly drove along. It seemed particularly brilliant in the sunshine as we passed the drab camouflage of Stoke Newington Town Hall. The crowds lining the route were all laughing and cheering as they waved flags and I expect that a little girl, who later became famous, was there too. She was Barbara Deeks, eight years old, now known as Barbara Windsor, and the star of 'Madame Behenna's Juvenile Jollities' even then.*

The spring weather that year was very similar to 65 years later, unreliable, but at least the sun shone for the Victory Procession, and it remained dry, but cloudy, when we had our street party. Long trestle tables were lined up, covered with sheets, and benches appeared. Women sashayed in and out of houses with dried egg and cress and Spam sandwiches piled high on plates and all the children tucked in before cakes, sprinkled with brightly coloured 'bits', appeared. On reflection, goodness knows where all the food came from, particularly the cakes, because rationing was very strict then, but my father was a baker so I suspect he provided the cakes. (His name might ring a bell with more mature readers. My father and his brother had six bakers' shops, Holgate's Bakeries, in the Stoke Newington and Tottenham area just after the war.) Orange squash or 'lemonade', very weak, or water was given to the children to drink, but in the evening I remember, when the tables had been cleared, men holding mugs of beer and listening to someone playing a piano that had been dragged into the street, and watching some of the grownups dance as dusk fell, but I have no photographs from that period. My husband has reminded me that film was practically unobtainable then. He had been given some sort of camera with ersatz film when he was 12 and remembers going on a bus down to Whitechapel to see a Victory Parade. He managed to get a photograph of Viscount Montgomery, which promptly faded. Unfortunately that's all he remembers about it. But then, he wasn't dancing about on a lorry!"

Pam married Alan Eaves in 1955. They now have two grown-up sons and two small grandsons, fortunately all living in fairly close proximity to them in the Epping Forest area of Essex. After working as a legal secretary for many years Pam began creative writing when she retired, and has had stories and articles published, as well as a book, "Light in the Shade", published by Circaidy Gregory Press in 2008. Pam also paints, and her work can be seen on www.pameaves.co.uk

Mark Rickman

Mark in retirement years

In common with most ex-servicemen, author and poet Mark Rickman is unwilling to go into detail about the more harrowing aspects of his wartime experiences. But in two of his poems, which appear at the end of this piece he reveals something of the horrors of war. Mark joined the army in 1943 when he was 18 years old.

"My first regiment was the Sherwood Foresters, where new recruits were told that when challenged with 'Are you Robin Hood?' we had to admit to being Robbing Bastards. I said I'd bear it in mind. Because I was taught to climb a rope using hands and feet at school, I became a physical training instructor. I know it sounds daft but I was the only one who could carry equipment up a rope without falling off. I volunteered for the paras, did my jumps at Ringway, Manchester, was sent to India, put in gliders in the Army Air Corps and because there weren't enough of them, became a section sergeant as part of the PBI (Poor Bloody Infantry.)

I left India on Independence Day, Aug 15th 1947, the day Pakistan came into existence and another war started over a line drawn across a map; all right, when it comes to borders I admit I have attitude. I got home to find I didn't have one. My parents were divorced and remarried and fully occupied with their new relationships. I took my kit to the Waterloo Club, an army club near Westminster Bridge, listened to Big Ben, put on my grey demob suit and, knowing the area, found lodgings in Seven Sisters Road. There were lots of jobs about and because I didn't care what I did to earn a crust, I found a job as a salesman in the Times Furnishing Company. By chance we loaned some furniture to the Finsbury Park Empire who were rehearsing a costume drama that included period uniforms. I had a word with the designer and began working on theatrical costumes. I had become interested in military history and uniforms during my period of service in South East Asia Command. This led to work on costumes and equipment for films and TV productions such as Beckett, A Man for All Seasons, The Charge of the Light Brigade, Camelot, Elizabeth R and Doctor Who. I worked hard because I refused to look back. Not at my parents, not at the war in the Far East. Not at the fact I never got the chance to kill Germans. Not at the dent in my head and not at the mess inside my head. What a time to get married! But I did and when I had too much to drink and began to rant, my wife, Dinah, threatened me with a bucket of water. Years later, she said I always asked if it was going to be cold or hot water and that saved our marriage. Thanks to her, I became reconciled with my parents and got rid of some of the angst I still carry but can switch off. Dinah died far too young but I had her long enough to restore my sanity; thankfully our two boys take after her."

Retiring in his fifties, Mark Rickman wrote short stories and articles for family and writers' magazines as well as plays, going on to be short listed and winning prizes in a number of literary competitions and gaining recognition abroad. He says of his poem "Wound Stripes", later re-titled "Delirium" that he has re-written it a number of times. Mark explained that wound stripes were small, gold colour metal strips attached to the sleeve of the uniform tunic, concluding, with typical candour, *"Big deal."*

WOUND STRIPE

I open one eye.
Above me shines a light.
The wrong shape,
wrong colour,
wrong intensity,
wrong memory.

I close the eye

and sink back
to exploded shell and
sudden lift from the Irrawaddy.

I fly and fall.
Fly and fall again
and again until
upon the river bank,
Mud is caking
whatever limp thing
is left of me.
My tongue
feels broken teeth.
A gob of blood,
while flies explore
the gape of my mouth.

I forget legs,
I forget arms,
while bloodied fingers
claw me back.
In the river
I drift downstream
at one with broken weed.

Shells and guns
explode round me.
A voice says:
'Time to wake up.'

I open one eye.
Above me is a face,
rosy red.
Her peeling nose
framed by cap and
loosened hair.

Sunburn, I remember,
is a self inflicted wound.
I could put her on a charge.

I try telling the silly bitch
but a dead fish floats by.

The nurse shakes my shoulder,
pats down my pointing finger,
and tells the doctor I am delirious.

Of course you are, says the fish
as it bellies up beneath the weed.
That's what you get for playing soldiers.

Mark says that "Sniper" was based on what the men were told while on patrol in Burma; he imagined the event depicted in the poem.

SNIPER
I stood tremble kneed, ankle deep
in rotting vegetation,
hearing the broken nosed sergeant,
who did not survive the action,
say *watch the trees for snipers*
who use their country's flag
to tie themselves to the branch they sit on
while waiting for an enemy to kill.

What do they want to do a daft thing like that for, Sarge?

He pats me on the shoulder
In the hope that when it's their time to die,
they remain upon their branch
and continue to serve their Emperor
by making us waste our bullets
and give away our position to their comrades.

Blimey Sarge, who's going to fall for an old trick like that?

Me, of course.
Convinced the sniper's eye was on me,
his rifle aimed.

I ignored the warning shouts and fired
and fired and fired again,
dislodging the weeks old corpse,
following it and its flag down through the branches
until it lay wet and triumphant.
Grinning up at me, while answering bullets
destroyed the platoon,
And the sergeant with the broken nose.

Everyone but me and the sniper's rifle
For ever trained upon my chest.

John Douglas Smith

War hero John Douglas Smith, remembered on Hastings War Memorial

Hastings author Marilyn Saklatvala recounts the story of her late uncle, John Douglas Smith, a 21 year-old pilot officer and her mother's brother. At one time his family lived at 44, High Street; it was bombed in May 1943, after they had moved house. John's death occurred a year before Mary was born but her elder sister remembers him coming home on leave on one occasion. Marilyn later understood her uncle to have been shot down and that he was recorded as "missing." She used to fantasise about his turning up, or tracing him when she was older, or at least, finding where he died. At the time of his death he was the navigator on Hampden No AT.138, which took off from Afrikanda, but was shot down near Aelekerti on the Russian/Finnish border.

"One day in August 1993, my husband said to me 'You know that plane they've found in Russia, (it had been on the news the night before), I think that is your Uncle John's plane.' My husband is interested in aviation history and knew the plane had been a Handley Page Hampden, known as

"the flying suitcase" because it had a truncated, narrow and tall main fuselage, with a very slender tail unit, resulting in cramped crew conditions. The day following the news of the plane's discovery, my husband rang RAF Brize Norton and confirmed that it was indeed my uncle's plane. He was told that the RAF had tried to contact relatives and some of them were travelling from as far away as Australia and Canada for the burial, which was to take place in Archangel, Russia, at the Allied Cemetery. We learned that my mother's cousins would be attending the funeral, but it was too late to arrange for us to take part. For the next few days the national press was full of the story, the most detailed report being in the Daily Mail of Tuesday, 24th August 1993. From this, with some background information from the RAF, we formed a better picture of what had taken place. It emerged that on the night of 4th September 1942, a mixed flight of 12 aircraft took off from Sumburgh, in the Shetlands, for North Russia, where their role was to be the protection of a convoy carrying vital weapons, to hold the German forces massed on the Eastern Front. They were to establish a base to protect the convoy as it arrived in Murmansk. According to the Daily Mail report, all were volunteers because it was accepted that many of them would probably never return.

Several aircraft were lost en route and one of these was Hampden AT138 of No 144 Squadron, which was attacked by enemy fighters. Four of the five man crew were killed, the pilot, John Bray, survived, bailing out shortly before the blazing aircraft crashed at Alakurtti, Lake Vikurij, Northern Finland. Alakurtti was formerly a Finnish village that was ceded to the Soviet Union after the Second World War.

My late mother had told me that contemporary reports said John Bray was captured by the Germans and the remains of the four crew members found in the wreckage were buried with full military honours. This was according to what John Bray was told by his German captors at the time. But post-war investigations by the Russian authorities failed to discover the graves. So it remained, with the names inscribed on the Runnymede memorial as 'missing in action, no known grave.' Until 1991, when the British Embassy in Moscow were informed that the wreckage of a British bomber of the Hampden type, and believed to be AT138, had been found together with human remains, fourteen kilometres from Alakurtti. In late August 1992, after several delays, officials from the Air Attaché's office were allowed to inspect the wreckage but couldn't positively identify the aircraft. One member of the crew had been thrown clear and he wore a ring, bearing initials, which were linked to a crew member with the same initials; from this Greater Manchester Police managed to trace his sister to Australia. She was sent a photo of the ring and was able to positively identify it, thus leading to the identification of the plane and remaining crew members. A former member of the same squadron recounted, at the time of the burials, how six planes went missing in the same period that an air search was carried out, locating three of the planes, but not the others. The searchers were hungry, and continuously under fire. Eventually they landed and continued the search on foot, but unsuccessfully. What I found particularly poignant are the details in the Daily Express, apparently taken from a report written for the Air Ministry by the surviving pilot:

'As the Hampden emerged from cloud over a German fighter base in the north of occupied Finland, two Messerschmitt BF109 fighters came up behind and beneath. In the Hampden, rear gunner Roy Otter must have seen them coming at him. A burst of enemy fire hit the rear of the plane; fire broke out... the crew members there probably died very quickly. From the front of the plane, navigator John Smith tried to crawl back with extinguishers to help his friends but the fire was too intense. Before he could get back to his seat, a second burst of shells and bullets hit the centre of the fuselage and he was a casualty. The fire was now raging throughout the plane and with only pilot John Bray left alive, the blazing Hampden fell into a spin.'" Marilyn added that if she needed further reminders of her Uncle John, his name is inscribed on the War Memorial in Hastings' Alexander Park.

Recalling her childhood and wartime memories she said that she believes she was destined to be a writer: *"I was born during the war in 'Oaklands', St Helen's Park Road, Hastings, which, as I discovered recently, was the family home of Dr Deeping, father of Warwick Deeping, novelist and short story writer. The house no longer seems to exist but was above Hillside Road. It's likely that it had been bequeathed to Warwick Deeping and was probably empty when he offered the house for use as a nursing home during WWII. My parents and my three siblings emigrated to Australia 1948, when I was aged four and a half. We sailed on the Egyptian ship 'El Misr', which we children called 'The Measles.' Although we settled in a very English-seeming area of Tasmania, I never felt that I belonged in Australia and returned to England aged 21. I went back to Australia in 1965, just a few weeks before the family home was engulfed by bushfires that destroyed everything we owned. After another short-term stay in England I married in 1970 and my husband and I went to Australia and remained there to raise a family. My personal memories of the war are those of a very young child. I was not sure of their being real until I was able to verify them years later. I recall being in bed, hearing what sounded like an air raid starting and my elder sister telling me to stay put, while she went to ask to ask my mother if we should go to the shelter. My father was away in the services at the time. I also remember the bomb sites. As to what effect the war had on my mother: I do not remember her speaking about it but I do know that she hated parsnips, as they were often used to bulk out wartime recipes; the same went for quinces. I think that my mother, like her brother John, was a very brave person. She demonstrated this when she and I set out to walk through bushfires in Tasmania, to get to my little sister, who was in the community of Snug."*

Andre Palfrey-Martin

Andre on a steamer trip with his father in the 1950s

Andre, born in 1947, grew up with a lively awareness of the war that had afflicted the previous generation. *"My friends and I played war games, with the British fighting the Germans; we regarded the war we had just missed as a great adventure. It was only as I grew older that I came understand how lucky I was to have escaped it. I do think that the generation that preceded mine value living, in a way that those of us following do not comprehend. When I was about 2 years old my family moved into one of the first prefabricated houses in Lewis Road, I recall that these temporary houses were very well appointed, with features that were luxuries at the time, including fridges and immersion heaters. My family took in a lodger for six months, a Polish ex-army captain who was working on phase two of the Hollington Housing Estate at the rear of Lewis Road; (The Communist regime in Poland made the former soldier's return home out of the question at the time) the prefab estate was a neighbourly community. Then my father bought a bombed site in Clyde Road for £100 and built a house on it, in which I live today."*

Andre saw something very interesting about 48 years ago, whilst he was a pupil at the Grove School for Boys, in the stables that were attached to a house called The Grove, long since demolished: *"During WWII the house and grounds had been used to accommodate German prisoners of war; in the stable there were instructions about switching off lights in German as well as murals painted by the POWs."* At one time Andre worked at Ore Place, the former Jesuit seminary that became the Army Records Office during the war and long after: *"Ore Place was never bombed during the war; local legend has it that because the building was constructed in the shape of a cross and clearly visible to aircraft, the Germans left it alone out of respect or superstition. But the explanation is more banal; the Germans lined up Christ Church in St Leonards, St John's Church, St Leonards and Ore Place as the navigation points to turn towards London."*

For the past 20 years Andre has been teaching History and Tourism in both Further and Higher Education. He is very involved in the community via the Gensing and Central St Leonards Community Forum, chairing the special interest group on Education and Young People. His other areas of commitment are the with the National Trust, on the Bodiam Castle management committee, the Nautical Heritage Association and at Christ Church St Leonards, where he has been an active member of the church community for well over 55 years.

Jana Tanner

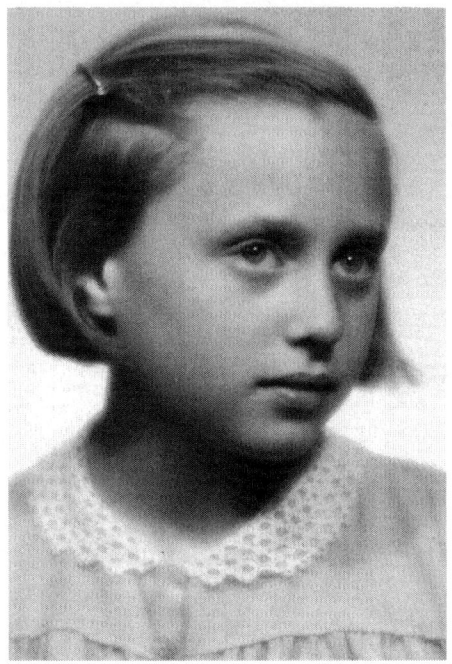

Jana Tanner, circa 1943

Jana was unusual in being a female in the post-war transportations; these consisted for the most part of boys. As Martin Gilbert writes in his book, "The Boys ~ the Story of 732 Young Concentration Camp Survivors" *'Girls and little children, unless they had been hidden from the Nazis for several years and not betrayed, died so easily.'* Here, Jana tells the story of her tragic childhood. "*During the last year of the war I was an inmate in an orphanage in Modra, a small town in Slovakia. (I was then fourteen years old). My parents arranged for me to be hidden in the Lutheran orphanage. With my two brothers my mother and father were deported to Nazi concentration camps; I escaped deportation because I was hidden. The head of the orphanage was the local Lutheran Pastor Julius Derer. To my knowledge there were at least six and probably more Jewish girls there at any one time; one Jewish boy was employed in the garden and a Jewish woman was working as a seamstress. In the same town was a Lutheran boarding school for girls where there were also several Jewish girls. However, these were informed on and arrested. Pastor Derer pleaded with the authorities, saying he considered himself in loco parentis, thus putting himself and his family in danger, but to no avail. Those of us hiding in the orphanage remained safe. The nuns who ran the orphanage treated us no differently from the other children, although our presence endangered their safety and must have put a strain on their housekeeping as they could not draw rations for us 'illegals.'*

On Easter Saturday 1945 the Russian Army fought its way into Modra, the Russians made the town their headquarters and all the inhabitants had to be evacuated. The orphanage was re-housed in a nearby village school, where the accommodation was very cramped; one large classroom became a dormitory for the girls (two to a bed) and the other one for the boys. Cooking was done in vats in the yard. We ate either standing up or sitting on the stairs. One of our teachers asked the orphanage for a suitable girl to help look after her sister's baby and I jumped at the opportunity of getting away. On VE day the whole village was celebrating with partying in the streets, bands playing, church bells ringing, and there was the unexpected sight of the vicar toasting the red army. For days after the end of the war I listened whenever I could to the radio, where all day they broadcast appeals from returning survivors looking for their families. Unfortunately my parents were not among them. The parents of my friends (two sisters) did come back and took me to live with them until August 1945, when my older sister, resident in England, arranged for me and my one surviving brother to join her. We travelled to England by a special transport of war orphans and were taken to Windermere where we stayed at a hostel.

The staff members there were not very understanding of our needs and they spoke Yiddish, which I did not understand. They thought that organised games were the way to help us but because we had become so institutionalised what we needed was individual human contact. In the hostel we were given bread and jam, such a luxury for us. The English people were saying that the bread was poor and grey-looking but to me it looked white and was so soft. We were also given ice cream, which I thought delicious. I later went to London, where my sister had lived since her marriage in 1939, and studied English at Regent Street Polytechnic; it was a special course for foreigners. Arriving in Britain was a great culture shock; there were so many people and everything seemed wonderfully new and free. The loss of my parents and most of my family at such a young age affected me deeply for much of my life. My mother was a very upright woman and taught us to tell the truth; it was painful to me as child and teenager to live a life that was a lie; hiding my Jewish birth and pretending my parents were dead, in order to protect myself."

The Slow Turning Tide

Written & compiled by Victoria Seymour

Victoria Seymour's The Slow Turning Tide looks back to over a half a century ago, when Hastings and St Leonards faced the long task of recovering from WWII. With her talent for uncovering intriguing detail Victoria features stories of Hastings citizens, rebuilding their lives, homes and careers, marrying and raising families, while enduring austerity and nine post-war years of rationing and shortage of everything, including houses.

Peacetime Hastings was the scene of two conflicts - the developers against the preservationists and the down-to-earth holiday traders opposing the die-hards, who yearned to see the town established as a select residential and coastal resort, a pre-war ideal that never really existed. In spite of controversy, Hastings soon reasserted itself as a popular holiday spot with a round of carnivals, processions, stage shows, galas, beauty contests and all the fun of the seaside.

Throughout the book the commentator on post-war news is Frederick Goodsell, the editor of the Hastings and St Leonards Observer and also its weekly columnist under the pen name "Vigilant". Goodsell, seeming part Churchill, part Mr Pooter, rails against the evils of progress and what he sees as the declining moral values of his town.

ISBN 0-9543901-6-7
www.victoriaseymour.com

Letters from Lavender Cottage

by Victoria Seymour

Hastings in WWII and Austerity

A collection of recently discovered letters, posted from Hastings to Canada between 1942 and 1955, inspired Victoria Seymour to compile a part-biography of their writer, Emilie Crane.

In her retirement, Emilie shared a house in Hastings, England, with her two friends, Clare and Edith and their much-loved cat, James. The almost one hundred letters Emilie sent to her Canadian cousins were initially of thanks for the food parcels they had supplied to the Lavender Cottage household in WWII and throughout the following years of harsh austerity. The letters also detail the lively and kind-hearted Emilie Crane's domestic and personal life and follow the joint fortunes of the three ageing women.

Victoria Seymour has rounded the story by adding contemporary national, local and autobiographical material. "Letters From Lavender Cottage" is a touching, human story with an informative narrative.

ISBN: 0-9543901-0-5   www.victoriaseymour.com

The Long Road to Lavender Cottage
written & compiled by Victoria Seymour

The now famous occupant of Lavender Cottage, Emilie Crane, returns, to let us back into her life and the daily doings of her neighbours on the Ridge. What was the truth about the supposed nudist colony opposite Lavender Cottage? Was the guest house close by really a haven for left wing agitators and a bolt hole for a scandalous occultist, Aleister Crowley?

Victoria Seymour has meticulously researched the background and history of a period and place that was peopled not just by locals leading ordinary lives but by notable figures from the worlds of literature, religion, the arts, healing, politics and entertainment, including Joanna Lumley.

We are given glimpses into the Ridge's former large Victorian houses, cottages, farms, institutions and businesses and the lives of their occupants in peace time and war. The Long Road to Lavender Cottage also reveals dramatic events in Emilie Crane's daily life that she was not able to write about in her wartime letters, for fear of the government censor.

ISBN: 0-9543901-4-8   www.victoriaseymour.com

Austerity Diary from Lavender Cottage Hastings 1947

Written and Compiled by Victoria Seymour

In this diary the now famous Lavender Cottage occupant, Miss Emilie Crane, reveals intimate details of her daily life, giving us a picture of how one household managed during the depths of the austerity period that followed WWII.

With the same cheerful stoicism that was part of the war effort, Emilie continued to 'make do' and follow the government's strict regulations on salvaging, (recycling), that give lessons to the 21st Century. The wartime spirit of all being in it together still lingered but Miss Crane found time for sedate amusements and discreet gossip about neighbours.

As well as a wealth of the local history details beloved by Victoria Seymour's readers, the diary contains austerity recipes and kitchen, gardening and household hints, making it the perfect bedside book.

Of Victoria's social histories Joanna Lumley said.

"I can't put Victoria Seymour's books down. They're just delightful and enthralling, a part of history which, unless she had preserved it, might have blown away like sand in the desert."

ISBN 978-0-9543901-7-4

Letters to Hannah

written & compiled by Victoria Seymour

WWII Recollections of Hastings & South East England

Letters to Hannah looks at WWII on the Home Front through the eyes of those who lived in Hastings and South East England from September 1939 to December 1945. It also enlarges on the historical background covered in its companion book, Letters from Lavender Cottage.

Letters to Hannah visits the lives of ordinary people, who endured extraordinary times. Among many others is the account of a Battle lad, born in a cottage beside the famous 1066 battlefield. Aged fifteen he enlisted as a Home Guard, the youngest member in the country at that time, a Hastings, wartime milk delivery girl details her working and family life under fire and a young first aid volunteer highlights the horrors of bomb and machine gun attacks on civilians. 'Letters to Hannah' is rich in anecdotes and information on food rationing and shortages, the blackout, air raids, population evacuation and civil defence. The book provides a moving and factual account of wartime Hastings, the town which features in the ITV, WWII detective fiction series, Foyle's War.

Victoria Seymour links this, her second WWII social history, with a series of autobiographical letters to the future, describing her war-troubled childhood to her newborn, 21st century granddaughter, Hannah. Extracts from Letters to Hannah were included in the BBC Radio 4 history series, The Archive Hour, in July 2003.

ISBN: 0-9543901-1-3   www.victoriaseymour.com

Court in the Act

written & compiled by Victoria Seymour

Crime and Policing in WWII Hastings
Foreword by Ann Widdecombe M.P.

Victoria Seymour's Court in the Act, which completes her trilogy, concentrates on the work of the police force, the magistrates' and other courts in WWII Hastings. As the effects of war took hold, there was hardly any aspect of home front life that was not controlled by some Government Act, Regulation or Order, putting even more pressure on already overworked police officers.

There passed before the courts a parade of 'spies', aliens, pacifists, looters, wartime racketeers and small-time criminals. Added to these were thousands of usually law-abiding people who found themselves in court for flouting often not properly understood laws. Sentences were handed down that sounded like something out of 19th Century history: A fine for stealing one onion from an allotment, a few apples from a tree or vegetable peelings from a dustbin or a month in prison for allowing light to escape from behind a curtain.

Meanwhile, the formidable Government Enforcers stalked the land incognito, seeking to trap unwary traders and citizens and bring them to justice. Police Court reports from the period 1939 to 1945 give an insight into a little discussed aspect of WWII. 'Vigilant', The Hastings and St Leonards Observer 1940s columnist, provides a background, with comment on the foibles and morals of a seaside town under fire.

Fact met fiction, when in 2004 Victoria Seymour was asked by Greenlit Productions, who film Foyle's War, the WWII detective television drama set in Hastings, to assist in re-creating a Hastings' wartime magistrates' court for series three.

ISBN: 0-9543901-2-1   www.victoriaseymour.com

HOST FAMILIES WANTED

Written & compiled
by Victoria Seymour

For over half century Hastings has been host to hundreds of thousands of young people from all over the world.

Host Families Wanted, the true story of overseas English language students in Hastings, is approached with the enthusiasm for detail that Victoria Seymour's regular readers expect of her.

She recounts her own experiences as student host mother, the company director of a family-run, Hastings based language school and how the work affected her life and family.

The problem of street offences against students is considered, as are the efforts of the police and the local authority to reduce the crime and protect students.

To enrich the story there are interviews with local host families and the students' teachers. In a set of essays, a group of today's overseas students comment frankly on Hastings and their hosts.

If you are a host family, have been, or are thinking of becoming one, this book is for you.

ISBN: 0-9543901-5-6
www.victoriaseymour.com